WEAVING FAITH FAMILY...

&

When You're Hanging on by a Thread!

WEAVING FAITH FAMILY...
&
When You're Hanging on by a Thread!

Reflections & Suggestions for Your Busy Family

Eileen Marx

ave maria press   Notre Dame, IN

To my husband, Joe,
my children, Bobby and Teresa,
and my faithful friend,
Fran

© 1999 by Ave Maria Press, Inc.

International Standard Book Number: 0-87793-685-4

Cover illustration and text design by Brian C. Conley

Printed and bound in the United States of America.

Library of Congress Cataloging-in-Publication Data

Marx, Eileen.
    Weaving faith and family : reflections and suggestions for your busy family / Eileen Marx.
          p.   cm.
    Includes index.
    ISBN 0-87793-685-4 (pbk.)
    1. Family—Religious life.   2. Family—Religious aspects—Catholic Church.
3. Christian education of children.   I. Title.
    BX2351.M374   1999
    249—dc21

                                                                99-31402
                                                                CIP

Contents

Introduction

There comes a moment in almost every parent's life when their children begin to ask them questions about God, heaven, and "what our family believes." Because children are so curious, open, and genuine, their questions often breathe new life into our faith.

During the past nine years, our children's questions, insights, and observations were often invitations to share something about our faith. Questions like these started my family's faith journey and became the inspiration for this book:

"If Jesus isn't dead anymore, why is he still on the cross?"

"If Jesus was Jewish, why don't we celebrate Hanukkah?"

"Does God tell the flowers to start blooming or do they just know to start?"

"Do you think it rains in heaven?"

"What do you think it smells like there?"

"If God is always right next to me, why doesn't He answer when I say 'hi' to Him?"

We are the most important teachers of the faith to our children. But my husband, Joe, and I believe that our children are also teachers of the faith to us, often leading us to God in ways we never could have imagined. To be close to the heart of a child is to be close to the heart of God.

A few years ago I started teaching a religious education class and I found that fifth graders have a lot to teach the rest of us. For example, during a discussion on heaven and eternal life, ten-year-old Joey spoke up: "Two things, Mrs. Marx. The first is that I think you're right. Jesus is just as sad as we are when someone we love dies. The second is that I think Jesus must also be really happy after someone dies because for the first time ever he's going to meet the person he created face to face. And that's going to be unbelievable!"

The faith I have today is so much richer and alive because of my children. But the journey hasn't always been easy. For almost five years I didn't go to church, except at Christmas and Easter. I don't think I ever stopped believing in God, but my faith was just slowly slipping away. Then, a few weeks after I graduated from college, I became the victim of a violent crime. Throughout this painful period, I gradually came to see that God would use the little faith I had and help me understand that even though I had let go of God, he would never let go of me.

During the years that followed, I eventually served as an advisor and communications director for Cardinal James Hickey in Washington, D.C. I had the opportunity to see the church up close and personal and meet many wonderful priests, sisters, and lay people. But it wasn't until my husband, Joe, and I had our two children, Bobby and Teresa, that my faith became a faith of the heart. After becoming a parent, it was so much easier to understand how God could love us no matter what we had done in our lives. One of the great blessings of having children is that you can rediscover and renew your faith through the eyes of your children.

Like many of today's families, we rush too much and pray too little. As parents, Joe and I start out with the best of intentions for our family and end up with the worst feelings of guilt and failure when we don't measure up to our own ideals and expectations. We try hard to say just the right words when our kids have had a bad day, when most of the time they simply want us to listen. At these moments, we don't always have our faith at our fingertips. We're so busy juggling families, careers, and countless other activities—all the while seeking to connect our faith to our busy lives.

We never know when an opportunity for sharing faith with our kids will come up—a friend's or family member's diagnosis of cancer, an argument at school or at home, a news story about a school shooting, or just the events and surprises that each day brings. During these moments, it takes a lot of time to locate just the right book on the subject, or to find the best family activity, or to search for that fitting Scripture quotation. It is my hope that having this information about our faith at your fingertips will help you and your family during these times and throughout the year.

Weaving Faith and Family . . . When You're Hanging on by a Thread! includes a reflection for each week of the year. Many of the reflections are columns I have written for newspapers or for RENEW 2000 during the past six years. Some are stories of how our faith deepened during the significant moments in our family's life—a miscarriage, the birth of our children, the first day of school, a traumatic sledding accident, and the illnesses and deaths of beloved family members and friends. But most of the stories center around how we try to connect our faith to the joys, sorrows, struggles, and challenges of everyday family life.

In addition to the story, each week contains six sections. The first, "In God's Words," includes scripture quotations on the theme of the week. The second section, "What Can a Family Do?" offers some practical family activities that are related to the topic and respectful of a family's busy schedule. The next two sections, "Books You Can Read with Your Children" and "Books and Resources for Parents," include quality books and resources for you and your children. The fifth section, "Conversation Starters," suggests questions to discuss at the kitchen table, in the car, or when you're tucking the kids in at night. The final "Prayer" is written or selected on the weekly theme.

You may wish to read the book one week at a time, or, if there is a specific issue you're interested in, you may want to look it up in the index.

Many of the suggestions and books in *Weaving Faith and Family . . . When You're Hanging on by a Thread!* have come from a large group of family members and friends. I had never thought to bless my children until my friend Fran told me how she blessed her children each evening before bed. I never knew how much kids enjoyed a guided meditation (with lights dimmed, music, and a candle burning) until Sister Carol encouraged me to try this with my fifth grade CCD students. I had never heard of a prayer table until my pastor, Father Vince, explained to parishioners how well these work in the home and during prayer services. It was my next door neighbor who recommended my all-time favorite Christmas book, *The Best Christmas Pageant Ever*. And truthfully, I never knew I was allowed to pick up a Bible and read it on my own until I joined a RENEW prayer group ten years ago.

Everyone's journey of faith is unique and there is a never ending list of resources, books, prayers, and activities that can help individuals and families along the way. I hope that you will visit our web page, **www.Faith-Family.com** and share your ideas, stories, favorite books, videos, music, and other resources with others. By doing this, we can help to build up our families and our churches as we spread our stories of faith.

I would also like to suggest three places that I have turned to many times as a parent. They consistently offer quality children's books, games, and resources: "Chinaberry: Books and Other Treasures for the Entire Family" at 1-800-776-2242; "Free Spirit: Works for Kids" at 1-800-735-7323; and "Hearth Song: A Catalog for Families" at 1-800-325-2502.

I have been so fortunate to have a remarkable group of friends and family members who trusted me to share their stories of faith and family throughout the pages of this book. To all of them I am so grateful. My greatest blessings, though, are my husband, Joe, my children, Bobby and Teresa, and my mother and father who have taught me the truest meanings of the words *faith* and *family*.

The First Week of January

January 1 is the beginning of the new year.

Creating Community

My daughter, Teresa, who was just weeks away from her fourth birthday, gently circled her arms around my neck and refused to let go of me any time we ventured out in our new town. Our family had recently moved to Lawrenceville, New Jersey, but Teresa and her brother, Bobby, had seen their old home dismantled then put back together again in a new house two hundred fifty miles away. We didn't have a friend or a guide to show us the way around our new community—only a poorly folded map on the front seat of the car and my miserable sense of direction.

We did manage to find our way to our new parish, St. Ann's, to drop off our parish registration form. The parish secretary was welcoming as she remarked that she thought we would be very happy in this area. As I told the secretary that so far we were really enjoying our new town, a head was lifted from my shoulder and Teresa said matter-of-factly, "Well, I'm not enjoying myself. I like my old school and my old church!" The secretary and I laughed, but secretly I was envious of my daughter's honesty and sympathetic with her confusion over all the unfamiliar people and places.

When we returned to the car, I wanted to tell Teresa that I wasn't exactly enjoying myself either. Creating community can be confusing, scary, and unsettling for parents and children. It's also hard work. Teresa's Uncle Ray said it best, "You're on a whole new playing field." We were starting from scratch hoping to find all the right ingredients.

But during those early days of our move, I sometimes wondered what were we really looking for in our neighborhood, school, and church? How would we define community and how would we know when we found it?

In God's Words

"You shall love your neighbor as yourself."

— Mark 12:31

"Which of these three, do you think, was a neighbor to the man who fell into the hands of the robbers?" He said, "The one who showed him mercy." Jesus said to him, "Go and do likewise."

— Luke 10:36-37

13

What Can a Family Do?

1. If you are planning a move, take a day in the new location just to help your children begin to get comfortable. Let them set the agenda.

2. Talk openly and honestly about the move. Don't be reluctant to share your own emotions.

We longed for a neighborhood where the neighbors were welcoming rather than suspicious. We prayed for a community that celebrated diversity and would speak out against hatred. We hoped to have neighbors of different cultures and religions so that we could grow in understanding. We wanted to live in a place where we could warm up the car on a cold morning and know it would still be there when we returned a few moments later. We wanted to live in a neighborhood where the wisdom of older residents was respected, where people organized to stop crime and to start block parties.

During the weeks following our move, I often heard the phrase, "Children are so adaptable; they'll adjust before you know it." As my daughter was "adjusting" by remaining in a constant state of clinging and nightly melt-downs and my son was "adapting" by running the Indy 500 around the living and dining room each evening, I wondered what I was doing wrong. But in my less vulnerable moments, I felt that maybe we had done something right. My children were out of sorts because they missed their old community with its security and happiness. I'm happy that they weren't quick to shed their loyalties. On some level I think they understood that you can only move forward once you've acknowledged what you've left behind.

Geri, a friendly "room mother" from my son's new kindergarten, called to welcome us to our new community. Geri said that she and her family had a similar adjustment problem when they moved from Brooklyn to Lawrenceville six months before. The first two months were unbearable for her son, Matthew, who spent most of the day crying. On the first day of school, Matthew's teacher asked him, "Where did you move from?" Matthew looked up and said, "Well, I used to live in America, but now I live in New Jersey."

There were days when I knew how Matthew felt. But as each day passed, I was also amazed at how, when you least expect it, a new community can begin to feel familiar, almost like home. Some days it only takes a friendly smile while picking up my children at school, an invitation to come over and play, a welcome from the parish priest after Mass, a "buddy" to show my son around his new school, or some reassuring words from an understanding teacher.

During that season of new beginnings for my family, I often thought about the importance of community and faith. In Matthew's Gospel, Jesus makes it clear that coming together as a community is at the heart of our faith: "For where two or three are gathered in my name, I am there among them" (Matthew 18:20). If we're not new to our communities, we have a responsibility to reach out to those who are. And we all are called, as a community of believers, to reach out to people in communities torn apart by drugs, poverty, crime, and neglect. Whenever we visit an elderly neighbor, babysit for a child of a single mother, or volunteer to help people in need, we are creating caring communities that help to build the kingdom of God.

One day a few weeks after we moved in, I picked up Teresa from a wonderful morning at her new nursery school. She said, "Mommy, I'm trying to get the thinking of my old school out of my head because it makes me a little sad and I had a happy time at my new school today." I told Teresa it was fine to keep that thinking in her head and in her heart—there will always be room for old friends and new friends. And then I wondered if perhaps this child who had been holding on to me for weeks was beginning to let go and enjoy her new community.

Books You Can Read with Your Children

Goodbye House
by Frank Asch

Alexander, Who's Not (Do You Hear Me? I Mean It!) Going to Move
by Judith Viorst

No Friends
by James Stevenson

The Berenstain Bears' New Neighbors
by Jan and Stan Berenstain

The Berenstain Bears' Moving Day
by Jan and Stan Berenstain

Cranberry Moving Day (Tales from Cranberryport)
by Wende and Harry Devlin

Oh, the Places You'll Go!
by Dr. Seuss

Books and Resources for Parents

Dave Barry's Homes and Other Black Holes
by Dave Barry

No Place Like Home: Rooms and Reflections From One Family's Life
by Linda Weltner

Conversation Starters

1. Think of a time when you started something new—the first day of school, the first night in your new home, the time you met a new friend. How did you feel? Who helped you during this time? What did they do? How do you feel about this new experience now?

2. If you could move anywhere, where would it be? Why? What's special about the place you're living in now? If you could change one thing about your community, what would it be?

3. Who does God tell us our neighbors are? How should we treat them?

Prayer

Lord, as we begin a new year, we recognize how difficult new beginnings can be. Help us to see the importance of friends, neighbors, and community throughout all the changes in our lives. May we be open to the new friends we will meet this year and the many possibilities we will discover for strengthening our church and community. As a family, help us to find ways to reach out to the people in our communities who are in need of our kindness, our time, and our prayers. Amen.

The Second Week of January

Mother Meltdown

A friend of mine was really letting me have it recently because I forgot about our plans. I tried to explain that sometimes there are so many activities and commitments that it's difficult to keep track of everything. These days, I feel fortunate when I show up at events even when they are written on my kitchen calendar, on a note pad by the phone, *and* on a Post-it® on my car's steering wheel. "How could you forget?" she asked. "You always seem to have it so together."

If this hadn't been such a tense moment in our argument, I would have asked her to write that last phrase down so my husband, Joe, would know that there was at least one person on this planet who thinks I have it together. She suggested that what I could really use was a daily planner listing appointments by the hour, a daily "To Do" list, and a page for monthly goals. I didn't have the heart to tell her that Joe gave me a day planner that I hardly used. I couldn't get beyond the first step: select an environment free from distractions.

I left my friend's house feeling depressed until I thought about a neighborhood baby shower I had been to recently for the mother-to-be of a third son. At the end of the party we all said how nice it was to visit with each other and to finally finish a sentence. We marveled at how a story that usually took ninety minutes to tell because of countless interruptions from our children could now be told in four minutes. We talked about how overwhelmed we were with the pace of life, all our children's activities, and the pressures not to slip up in our roles as wives, mothers, professionals, and volunteers.

The overload takes its toll emotionally, mentally, and physically. One mother said, "Has anyone ever asked you the name of your child and you momentarily draw a blank?" Another mother added, "Has

In God's Words

"As a mother comforts her child, so I will comfort you; you shall be comforted in Jerusalem."

— Isaiah 66:13

Meanwhile, standing near the cross of Jesus were his mother, and his mother's sister, Mary the wife of Cleopas, and Mary Magdalene. When Jesus saw his mother and the disciple whom he loved standing beside her, he said to his mother, "Woman, here is your son." Then he said to the disciple, "Here is your mother." And from that hour the disciple took her into his own home.

— John 19:25-27

What Can a Family Do?

1. Tell your children what it was like on the day they were born. What special memories do you have?

2. Talk about what it must have been like to be Mary, the Mother of God. Pray the "Hail Mary" together.

3. Read Tomie dePaolo's book *Mary: The Mother of Jesus* as a family.

4. Encourage your children to interview a grandmother, aunt, or older relative about what it was like to raise their children and how their faith guided them. Share their story with your family.

anyone asked you your *own* name and you draw a blank?" Then the mother who was being honored at the shower said, "Do you find your children correcting you when you repeatedly use the wrong words? The other day I kept saying, 'pick up the duck off the floor.' My son, Ryan, said, 'Mom, I think you mean pick up my jacket, don't you?'"

One mother sat quietly on the couch and finally spoke toward the end of the conversation. "I'm so relieved to hear everyone talking like this," she said. "I thought all of you had it so together and that I was the only one doing these things. I was getting ready to make an appointment with the neurologist, but now I understand I have nothing more than a case of mother meltdown."

These days, when the beep of the microwave nudges me to open its door, I have no idea what I put in there two minutes earlier. As we rush to get out of the house in the morning, my son suddenly remembers that he needs to bring in something to share for "Letter X Week!" My monthly goal is to be on time for just one event. My friend Fran often asks, "Is that a real half-hour or a Marx family half-hour?"

I used to have a memory that never failed. But those days are long gone. The day my memory began to go was the day I became a mother. I had to make room for all the memories of my children that continue to fill up my mind and heart. As my children are growing, I find that much of my own memory bank is filled up with remembering my children's upcoming school events, soccer practices, registration forms, and birthday party invitations. The loss of memory is just another casualty of caring for my children with love and intensity.

Whenever I'm having a "mother meltdown," I think it's important to reflect on the story of Martha and Mary. When Jesus arrives at the sisters' home, Mary sits at the feet of our Lord while Martha runs around seeing that all the preparations are made for their special guest.

My mother, who is a dedicated and involved mother of six, grandmother of twelve, coordinator of a Christian service program at a diocesan high school and a volunteer at the senior citizens' Dial-a-Ride, has often said that she never particularly liked the message of the story of Mary and Martha. Like most mothers, she identifies with Martha. "It would be wonderful to sit at Jesus' feet, but when Jesus gets hungry, who's going to take the turkey out of the oven?"

My mother not only understands, but follows the real message of the story of Mary and Martha. In the whirlwind of our lives we need to make time to sit at the feet of our Lord and listen to what he is asking us. We need to ask ourselves if prayer is listed first on our daily "To Do" list. Do we make appointments to help those in need? Do our personal and professional goals include deepening our spiritual life? The words that Jesus spoke in the home of Martha and Mary so many years ago are words spoken to us today in our harried and hurried homes, "You are worried and distracted by many things; there is need of only one thing. Mary has chosen the better part, which will not be taken away from her" (Luke 10:41-42).

Books You Can Read with Your Children

Are You My Mother?
by P.D. Eastman

Five Minutes' Peace
by Jill Murphy

A Chair for My Mother
by Vera Williams

Horton Hatches the Egg
by Dr. Seuss

The Way Mothers Are
by Miriam Schlein

On Mother's Lap
by Ann Herbert Scott

Jonathan and His Mommy
by Irene Smalls

Mama Bear
by Chyng Feng Sun

Owl Babies
by Martin Waddell

The Chalk Doll
by Charlotte Pomerantz

When Mama Comes Home Tonight
by Eileen Spinell

Books and Resources for Parents

Confessions of a Happily Organized Family
by Deniece Schofield

Confessions of an Organized Homemaker: The Secrets of Uncluttering Your Home and Taking Control of Your Life
by Deniece Schofield

Mother and Son Tales retold
by Josephine Evetts-Secker

Mother and Daughter Tales retold
by Josephine Evetts-Secker

For My Child: A Mother's Keepsake Journal
by Linda Kranz

Conversation Starters

1. I am thankful to God for my mother because. . . .

2. I am thankful to God for my child/children because. . . .

Prayer

The Hail Mary

Hail, Mary, full of grace,
the Lord is with you!
Blessed are you among women,
and blessed is the fruit of your womb,
Jesus.
Holy Mary, Mother of God,
pray for us sinners,
now and at the hour of our death. Amen.

The Third Week of January

January 21 is the anniversary of Roe v. Wade.

Abortion's Other Victims

The young woman spoke gently and sorrowfully as she told me about her abortion eight years ago.

"When I first found out I was pregnant, I was already twenty-one weeks along. I was twenty-two years old. I had been dating a young man for a while, but we were both too terrified to keep the baby. I am the middle daughter of a strong, traditional, Catholic family from the Midwest. My older sister had a child out of wedlock and I was the first daughter to go to college. I was afraid that my news would give my father a heart attack. I just couldn't disappoint my parents. More than anything else I was scared—scared that my relationship would fall apart, scared that my parents would find out, and scared that I was going to have an abortion.

"I remember when the abortion was over I felt an incredible sense of relief. But within a couple of months everything started to hit me. I began a downward spiral of self-destructive behavior. Some women turn to drugs or alcohol to get rid of the pain of their abortion. Others even contemplate suicide. I became very promiscuous. I had a string of broken relationships. I was going downhill quickly. I had nightmares and I was afraid to be by myself.

"Two years after the abortion God began placing things before me. I was at the library one day and a book on pregnancy fell open on the ground. It landed on the page that showed an unborn child at twenty-one weeks. Then my friend had a miscarriage at twenty-one weeks. Lots of things were bombarding me.

"Shortly afterward I moved to Washington and four years after the abortion I went on a Catholic retreat for young adults. It was the first time since the abortion that I went to confession. Confession

In God's Words

"Let anyone among you who is without sin be the first to throw a stone at her." And once again he bent down and wrote on the ground. When they heard it, they went away, one by one, beginning with the elders; and Jesus was left alone with the woman standing before him. Jesus straightened up and said to her, "Woman, where are they? Has no one condemned you?" She said, "No one, sir." And Jesus said, "Neither do I condemn you. Go your way, and from now on do not sin again."

—John 8:7-11

What Can a Family Do?

1. When you believe your children are old enough, talk to them openly about abortion from a faith perspective.

2. If you or a member of your family know someone who has had an abortion, pray for that person and for those who have been affected by the abortion.

3. When you talk to your older children about abortion, talk about the importance of reaching out to women in difficult pregnancies through prayer and support rather than sitting in judgment of another person's actions.

4. Read some of the gospel stories about forgiveness. Remind your children that God's forgiveness is always there; all that we need to do is ask for it.

was a big part of my healing. After the retreat my healing progressed."

Today this young woman is a volunteer at Project Rachel. She helps facilitate a support group in the Archdiocese of Washington. She also shares the experience of her abortion with seminarians and priests during their retreats so that they can better understand and assist women who are in need of post-abortion reconciliation.

This young woman told me that she felt called to Project Rachel. "I want to give to other women the mercy that God has shown to me. Post-abortion healing is not an easy process. It's very painful. God requires us to be honest with ourselves and to do some real soul searching. When you empty yourself and let God speak to you, that's when the real healing begins."

The first Project Rachel was founded by Vicki Thorn in the Archdiocese of Milwaukee in 1985. Today there are more than ninety Projects Rachel throughout the United States. Ms. Thorn said, "What many people don't realize is that back in 1975 when the U.S. bishops drafted their pastoral plan for pro-life activities, they not only called for pastoral outreach to women in crisis pregnancies, but also to those women broken by abortion. The bishops have been an incredibly prophetic voice in post-abortion reconciliation.

"Project Rachel is a message of hope and healing. Many times the effects of a woman's abortion surface seven to ten years later. At that point their lives are in a shambles. These women hang onto their pain because it's all they have left. At Project Rachel we invite people to grieve over their loss."

Ms. Thorn says that post-abortion healing is not just a process for women. "With abortion, there is a whole circle of impact, including fathers, grandparents, aunts, uncles, and cousins. They are the forgotten pieces in this. They need to know it's okay to grieve. Something very important was taken from their lives. It's normal and natural to grieve for what we've lost."

The young woman who lost her child eight years ago is a painful reminder of the personal and human dimensions of abortion. Her story is also a reminder that the only way we will really bring about change in the abortion debate is if our language of life is also a language of love and forgiveness. What if we followed the example of Project Rachel and offered a message of mercy to abortion's other victims? It seems that shouting harsh judgments and condemnations at women who have had abortions only serves to harden hearts rather than change them. What if women knew that when they experience anguish from abortion, the church will be there to ease their suffering and to give them the gift of God's mercy and love? I imagine that the women who are reconciled through Project Rachel experience God's forgiveness in a powerful way that most of us will never know.

As the young woman finished talking about her abortion and her reconciliation, she said, "Many women who have had an abortion feel they are evil and damned for all time. It becomes a self-fulfilling prophecy. But when they read scripture or go through post-abortion healing, they reconcile their broken relationship with God and understand that God loves them. He doesn't want them to destroy themselves. In their minds they know that God has forgiven them, but complete healing of their hearts doesn't happen until they are finally able to forgive themselves."

Project Rachel's Referral Line: 1-800-5-WE-CARE

Books You Can Read with Your Children

Red, Blue and Yellow Yarn: A Tale of Forgiveness
by Miriam Kosman

The Priest with Dirty Clothes: A Timeless Story of God's Love and Forgiveness
by R.C. Sproul

Learning About Forgiveness from the Life of Nelson Mandela
by Jeanne Strazzabosco

Jesus Forgives My Sins
by Mary Terese Donze, A.S.C.

Books and Resources for Parents

Psycho-Spiritual Healing After Abortion
by Douglas R. Crawford and Michael Mannion

A Path to Hope: For Parents of Aborted Children and Those Who Minister to Them
by John J. Dillon

Catholic Women and Abortion: Stories of Healing
by Pat King

Help for the Post-Abortion Woman
by Teri Reisser, M.S., and Paul Reisser, M.D.

Conversation Starters

1. Can you think of a time when you hurt another person? Were you forgiven? How did it feel?

2. Is there anything that is unforgivable? Will God forgive all that we've done wrong? What is the key ingredient for us to know true forgiveness?

Prayer

Merciful God, help us to be a family that reaches out to those in need through prayer and support, especially to young people who are in difficult pregnancies. May we avoid judging others and condemning them. Let our own homes be places where we forgive one another easily. Help us to remember the great need each of us has for forgiveness in our lives. We ask this through Christ our Lord. Amen.

The Fourth Week of January

A Sledding Story

Almost from the day my children were born, my husband and I have blessed them each evening with the prayer, "May God's angels watch over my angels." A few days before Christmas in 1995, God answered my prayer in a special way.

That year, on the Wednesday before Christmas, school was canceled because of a snowstorm. By late morning, a group of neighborhood children and parents had gathered at the park up the street from our house to go sledding. When I brought my son, Bobby, five and a half, and daughter, Teresa, three and a half, to join in the fun, I was told the hill was fine. But moments later, as Bobby headed down the hill on his first run, he hit an icy patch and spun head-first into a tree.

It is difficult and painful to describe the horror I felt as I turned Bobby over in the snow and saw a face I hardly recognized. His right eye was already swollen shut. As I held Bobby close and tried to comfort him, he cried out, "Mommy, Mommy."

During the next three days at Children's Hospital in Washington, D.C., being Bobby's "mommy" took me to frightening places—places in my heart where security no longer existed, where terror touched me as never before, and where I was overwhelmed with thoughts of "If only. . . ." Bobby sustained a skull fracture above his right eye that ran up along his forehead and very close to the base of his brain. He also sustained two orbital fractures, one small one just beneath his left eye and a larger one that ran from his left eye toward his temple. The second fracture came within a hair of severing the optic nerve, which would have cost him his sight in his left eye.

For three days Bobby was observed closely to make sure that the eye fracture would not cause a

In God's Words

And early in the morning he came walking toward them on the sea. But when the disciples saw him walking on the sea, they were terrified, saying, "It is a ghost!" And they cried out in fear. But immediately Jesus spoke to them and said, "Take heart, it is I; do not be afraid." Peter answered him, "Lord, if it is you, command me to come to you on the water." He said, "Come." So Peter got out of the boat, started walking on the water, and came toward Jesus. But when he noticed the strong wind, he became frightened, and beginning to sink, he cried out, "Lord, save me!" Jesus immediately reached out his hand and caught him, saying to him, "You of little faith, why did you doubt?" When they got into the boat, the wind ceased. And those in the boat worshiped him, saying, "Truly you are the son of God."

—Matthew 14:25-33

What Can a Family Do?

1. Set a good example by wearing helmets for bike riding and sledding.

2. As a family, talk about other rules of safety in your home—fire, strangers, dialing 911, etc.

3. As a family, watch the movie *Iron Will* (Walt Disney Pictures). It's a story that shows the courage and true heroism of a fatherless teenage boy during a dog sled race.

problem with the optic nerve. The attending neurosurgeon also wanted Bobby watched very closely because his CT-scans showed a cloudy spot in the brain area. If problems developed with either of these fractures the doctors would have to consider emergency surgery, a risky procedure.

Two days before Christmas we were blessed with the news that all Bobby's fractures were healing remarkably well and the injury did not cause any permanent damage. On Christmas morning, his swollen eye opened for the first time. In a season of miracles, we received the miracle of God giving our son back to us.

As I recall those first hours in the hospital, I know they were some of the darkest hours I've ever experienced. I wondered where God was as I was drowning in a world of medical terminology and procedures that were overwhelming and frightening. My family's safe and secure world seemed to be crashing in all around me. I felt like Peter as he tried to walk on water to meet Jesus during a storm at sea. He saw only the turbulent waters and felt the strong headwinds rather than seeing the outstretched arms of Jesus reaching for him across the sea. In the hospital I felt like I was being tossed about; I could see only the waves.

The morning of the accident was especially frightening to me because my husband, Joe, was in Princeton, New Jersey, where he had begun his new job three weeks earlier. Joe was stranded for six hours in the same snowstorm that had hit the Washington area. When Joe arrived in the emergency room, I knew that the only other person who shared the love and responsibility for Bobby as a parent was also there. Together, and with God's grace, we would find a way through the difficult days ahead. It was only a day or two later when I realized that not only were the hands of God reaching out to me, they caught me and held me close when I could hold on no longer.

God was everywhere during the first few days of Bobby's accident. He provided me with my son's calm and reassuring soccer coach who accompanied me during the first six hours we spent in the hospital and with two of my closest friends who cared for my daughter during the crisis. And then God sent my sister-in-law, who is a nurse, to give Bobby and me comfort and support until Joe arrived. The hand of God was at work in all the friends and family who called with prayers, love, and support, especially my mother, who came to help by bringing meals and her own special motherly love. We felt the presence of God when our pastor, Father Joseph Sileo, came to visit Bobby and bless him—a visit as important to us as any of Bobby's doctors. God's angels were in the twenty-six children from Bobby's kindergarten class who sent their love and get well wishes with home-made cards. God's compassion was in Dr. Hughes, a pediatric opthamologist who showed a real expertise in her field. She also showed my son a gentleness that we will never forget.

The times I felt God's presence more than any other were the times I looked at Bobby those first days in the hospital. Behind his bruised and swollen face was a brightness and bravery that I had never seen before. As Bobby endured a series of painful X-rays and tests, he never complained. He had gotten very sick before one of his CT-scans but to the amazement of the technicians, he remained calm as we pretended he was an Apollo 13 astronaut getting ready for his mission in space. When his good friend Will thought the accident was somehow his fault and began crying, Bobby smiled and said, "It wasn't your fault, Will; it was the tree's fault." In the early hours of the morning when I couldn't sleep, I climbed into Bobby's hospital bed just so I could hear his breathing. "You are my hero," I whispered to him.

In the weeks following the accident, my son of almost six years continued to teach the rest of us how to heal physically and emotionally. When our neighbor from across the street came to visit Bobby after his accident she said, "Bobby, I bet you'll never want to go sledding again!" "Oh no," Bobby said. "I still love to go sledding. I just hate to go crashing into trees!" May God's angels watch over all our angels.

Shortly after Bobby's injury, I read an Associated Press story in the *Washington Post* with the headline,

Books You Can Read with Your Children

The Bravest Dog Ever: The True Story of Balto
by Natalie Standiford

The Sled Surprise
by Kelli C. Foster and Gina Clegg Erickson

Snow
by Roy McKie and P.D. Eastman

Richard Scarry's Iciest Day Ever: A Pop-Up Book With Interactive Play Magnets
by Richard Scarry

The Snowy Day
by Ezra Jack Keats

Do the Angels Watch Close By?
by Mary Joslin

Books and Resources for Parents

Angels All Around Us
from Redemptorist Pastoral Communications

Conversation Starters

1. Have you ever been seriously hurt or very sick? What helped you to feel better? Were family and friends a part of the healing?

2. When do you think it's the hardest to "have faith?"

"Season's Sledding Injuries Hit Epidemic Proportions." The article stated that the Consumer Product Safety Commission estimates that 33,000 people a year in the United States, more than half younger than sixteen, require emergency room treatment because of sledding accidents.

After I read the article, I felt that we should do something to increase awareness about sledding safety. While Bobby was recuperating and needed "quiet time," we made sleds from Popsicle sticks, decorated them as Christmas ornaments and wrote, "Stay Safe on a Sled, Wear a Helmet on Your Head." We have given the sleds to our family and friends to pass along the message. The Director of my daughter's nursery school asked me how she could help. I asked her if she would put the message of our sleds in the school's newsletter.

A few weeks after Bobby's accident, I received a call from Lynn, the mother of one of my daughter's classmates. She was calling me from a local hospital to say thank you to Bobby. Lynn had read the article in the school's newsletter and had put a helmet on her son Matthew. While sledding earlier that afternoon Matt hit a metal handrail head-on and was rushed to the emergency room. While Matt would need to be observed for the next twenty-four hours, the doctors told Lynn that the helmet prevented a severe head injury or far worse.

Prayer

Traditional Guardian Angel Prayer

Angel of God, my guardian dear,
to whom God's love commits me here;
Ever this day be at my side,
to light and guard, to rule and guide.
Amen.

The First Week of February

February is Black History Month.

A Child Looks at Racism

One January morning when my son, Bobby, was four, he asked me, "Why don't I have to go to school today?" "Today is a school holiday. It's the birthday of Dr. Martin Luther King, Jr.," I answered him. "Who is Dr. Martin Luther King and why does he have a very long name?" Bobby pressed on.

I explained as simply as I could that a long time ago people who had black skin had to sit in the backs of buses, movie theaters, restaurants, and even churches, just because their skin was black. Those were the rules in the United States at that time. I told him that people were mean to people just because they had black skin. But Martin Luther King believed that everyone should learn to love one another and he told people we needed to change the rules. Another man thought Martin Luther King was wrong and he shot him with a gun and killed him.

Bobby looked at me as if I were making this all up. "Well, my friends Gerard and Rachel and Rocky and my Aunt Evelyn all have black skin and I think black skin is wonderful," he said earnestly. "So do I, Bobby," I replied. "It's different now," I continued. "All your friends, of all different colors, can play and go to school together." "I know that," he said. "Rachel likes to drink 'Sunny D' orange juice and so do I and she can come over to my house anytime and we can drink it together."

Throughout that day, Dr. King's name surfaced in both the simple and profound observations of a child: "What happened to Martin Luther King's children after he died? I see that Martin Luther King had a mustache. Did he get shot with a black gun or a brown gun? Even if people hated people with black skin, why did they still have to do mean things to them?"

In God's Words

Learn to do good; seek justice.

— Isaiah 1:17

Mighty King, lover of justice, you have established equity; you have executed justice and righteousness.

— Psalm 99:4

"Is not this the fast that I choose: to loose the bonds of injustice, to undo the thongs of the yoke, to let the oppressed go free, and to break every yoke?"

— Isaiah 58:6

What Can a Family Do?

1. Look for examples of racism in television, movies, and popular culture. Discuss them with your children.

2. Refuse to tolerate racial slurs or "jokes" in your home.

3. Read books with your children that celebrate different cultures.

4. Teach racial justice by your own example.

5. With your children, read about Moses or view the video *Prince of Egypt*—the story of a leader and his people who struggled for freedom from slavery.

As I talked with Bobby that day, I realized how racism and prejudice go against a child's natural inclination to embrace people and things that are different. Children are drawn to diversity. They delight in the many colors of the rainbow. Children see the possibilities in a box of sixty-four Crayolas. A child is colorblind when it comes to playmates. But somewhere along the way some children get the message that sameness is more desirable than diversity.

As my husband, Joe, and I talked later that evening, we spoke about how fortunate we both were in having parents who never lectured us about the evils of racism, but instead gave witness through their own words and example that prejudice and hatred would not be tolerated in their homes or in their hearts.

As a child I remember my mother and father working on a mayoral campaign for one of the few African-American residents in our town. I also remember hearing many stories over the years of my mother's friendship with her college roommate who happened to be black. The love and respect that they had for people of all cultures, races, and faiths flowed from their hearts. As my mother said, "If you feel that way in your mind and heart, it comes across to your children. You can't put one over on kids; they are very astute and they know hypocrisy when they see it."

For a few summers my family participated in a program run by Catholic Charities where a five-year-old boy named Lorenzo from Paterson, New Jersey, stayed with our family for two weeks during the summer. Lorenzo grabbed a piece of all our hearts and forever changed how we looked at racism. My mother told me, "We got involved in this program not because we thought we were do-gooders, but because we thought it would be a real opportunity to show you children that people of other cultures have gifts that will strengthen and enrich your lives. It's a two-way street."

I was ten years old in 1968 when Martin Luther King was assassinated. I remember being very confused about the bloodshed over race, but I sensed an urgency in my family and in my country that we must never allow hatred and violence to triumph over love and justice.

In February we celebrate Black History Month, and it's tempting to think that we have conquered racism. In many ways, the urgency and the passion of the Civil Rights movement appear to be gone, but the struggle against racism is far from over. The KKK still marches in U.S. cities. People in this country still commit unconscionable hate crimes against people of different cultures, races, and religions. And the denial of opportunities for African-Americans in our society has often resulted in what Washington Cardinal James A. Hickey calls "a new slavery of poverty, unemployment, and substance abuse."

As racism becomes more insidious, parents have an even greater responsibility to teach their children love, understanding, and respect for all people.

On a sunny, winter afternoon my husband and I watch Bobby and his friends playing happily at the park. We see their wonderful black skin and their wonderful white skin side by side and believe for a moment that a piece of Martin Luther King's dream has become a reality.

Books You Can Read with Your Children

Children Just Like Me: A Unique Celebration of Children Around the World
by Barnabas and Anabel Kindersley

Young Martin Luther King, Jr.: I Have a Dream
by Joanne Mattern
(A Troll First-Start Biography)

Wilma Unlimited: How Wilma Rudolph Became the World's Fastest Woman
by Kathleen Krull

Minty: A Story of Young Harriet Tubman
by Alan Schroeder

Bright Eyes, Brown Skin
by Cheryl Hudson and Bernette Ford

The Sneetches and Other Stories
by Dr. Seuss

Sister Anne's Hands
by Marybeth Lorbiecki

The Lotus Seed
by Sherry Garland

Ashanti to Zulu: African Traditions
by Margaret Musgrove

Her Stories: African American Folktales, Fairy Tales and True Tales
by Virginia Hamilton

Thank You, Jackie Robinson
by Barbara Cohen (Grades 3-6)

Roll of Thunder, Hear My Cry
by Mildred D. Taylor (Grades 4-6)

To Kill a Mockingbird
by Harper Lee

Books and Resources for Parents

Brothers and Sisters To Us: U.S. Bishops Pastoral Letter on Racism in Our Day
by the National Conference of Catholic Bishops (English and Spanish editions)

Parenting for Peace and Justice: Ten Years Later
by James and Kathleen McGinnis

Educating for Peace and Justice
by James and Kathleen McGinnis (3 volumes with teacher's manual) To order: (314) 533-4445.

Communities of Salt and Light: Reflections on the Social Mission of the Parish
by the National Conference of Catholic Bishops (English and Spanish editions)

Conversation Starters

1. Have you ever had a wish or a dream come true? How did it feel? Why do you think it came true?

2. Do you think that Dr. Martin Luther King, Jr., and Jesus had a similar dream? Can you think of anything that you and your family can do to keep Dr. King's dream alive today?

Prayer

"I have a dream that one day little black boys and black girls will be able to join hands with little white boys and white girls as sisters and brothers. I have a dream that my four little children one day will live in a nation where they will not be judged by the color of their skin but by the content of their character. I have a dream that one day the glory of the Lord will be revealed and all flesh shall see it together. I have a dream of freedom ringing from every mountaintop, from every hilltop. And when we allow freedom to ring from every state and city, we will be able to speed up that day when all of God's children will be able to join hands and say, 'Free at last, free at last, thank God almighty, we are free at last.'" Amen.

(Excerpts taken from Dr. Martin Luther King, Jr.'s "I Have A Dream" speech.)

The Second Week of February

Valentine's Day is February 14.

Hands of Love

"I met Bob in a drug store in 1933 while I was having a soda with my girlfriends, and I thought he was about the handsomest man I had ever seen," recalled my friend and neighbor Mary. "The first thing I noticed about him was his dark brown hands. He looked so strong! And when he first came to meet my mother, he showed up in a white suit and lavender tie. She told me, 'You had better hang on to that man!'"

Mary and Bob have been hanging on to each other for fifty-nine years. And for the seven years that my husband and I have known them, their marriage has been an inspiration to us. It is obvious to all who know them that they share a genuine love, a beautiful tenderness, and a deep respect for each other.

"We love and care about each other," said Mary. "We have fun no matter what we do. We would even have a good time going to the grocery store together. I think a good marriage has to have all these things. And you have to know how to hang loose through the good times and bad."

A few weeks ago, Bob suffered a stroke. One night after returning home from the hospital, Mary told me, "Bob looked so weak, his hands looked so pale. Our grandson was holding Bob's hands tonight and it was *his* hands that looked so strong and dark next to Bob's. My grandson reminded me so much of Bob as a young man."

As I listened to Mary talk I began to wonder if the love shared by Mary and Bob is a love from another time. Somehow life seemed a lot easier then. Falling in love was as simple as sharing an ice cream soda. But over the next few days, as Mary talked about the Depression, World War II, and the fear that her daughter might contract polio, I realized that

In God's Words

Love is patient; love is kind; love is not envious or boastful or arrogant or rude. It does not insist on its own way; it is not irritable or resentful; it does not rejoice in wrongdoing, but rejoices in the truth. It bears all things, believes all things, hopes all things, endures all things. Love never ends. . . . And now faith, hope and love abide, these three; and the greatest of these is love.

— 1 Corinthians 13:4-8, 13

"I give you a new commandment, that you love one another. Just as I have loved you, you also should love one another. By this everyone will know that you are my disciples, if you have love for one another."

— John 13:34-35

What Can a Family Do?

1. Make time as a couple to get away for an evening. If relatives don't live nearby, arrange to trade an evening of babysitting with good friends.

2. Look through your wedding album with your husband/wife and children. Tell your children the story of how you first met or when you knew you were falling in love.

3. Not everyone is easy to love. Say a prayer or try to find something good in a person who is difficult to get along with.

every generation has its concerns about the economy, its worries about illnesses without a cure, and its fears about war and poverty. It is how we respond to tragedies and challenges like these that helps to define who we are as a family and a society.

Today it seems that we try to control everything, even love. We need to figure it all out, have all the answers, find the perfect match, read the latest "How To" book, and wrap it up into a neat little package. Life is too stressful these days to spend the time working on a marriage or hanging in there for the long haul if times get too tough.

Maybe we are taking all the mystery out of love, and in the process we are losing sight of its real meaning. We often forget, I think, that God is there to guide us on our journey together. (I also believe that God is there to guide husbands or wives out of abusive or truly destructive marriages and give them strength during their time of grief and anguish.)

My former pastor and dear friend, Bishop William Curlin, once remarked that the primary vocation for a married couple is loving one another and building up Christ in each other. As a mother of two young children, this is an important reminder for me. Bishop Curlin says, "Live for one another and through your love you will reach out to your children, your community, and to people in need. Children don't make the marriage, they enrich it. When a husband and wife look at one another they should see the face of God because Jesus said he would live in each of us. What a price we are paying for losing sight of God in one another."

Once a month my husband and I try to get away for a romantic dinner, a picnic in the park or, if grandma and papa are willing, a cherished night away together. A married couple doesn't need to spend a lot of money to grow in a marriage, but they do need to spend time together. I think it's important to always rediscover the person you fell in love with before the kids arrived, before the fifty-hour work week became commonplace and before life somehow became all too stressful. If we take the time to put our marriages first, maybe we too will be blessed to hang in there for fifty-nine years.

Bob fought hard to overcome his illness, but eventually the stroke that had weakened him claimed his life. At his wake, as I knelt before his casket, I felt a gentle squeeze on my shoulder. "He would be so tickled if he knew you were here," Mary said. "I think he does, Mary," I whispered back. Fighting back tears, she said, "Enjoy and treasure every moment with that dear husband of yours; the years go by quicker than you think."

I noticed Bob's hands, they were pale and swollen. As if she were reading my thoughts, Mary said softly, "I tried to put his wedding ring on but his fingers were too swollen from his illness."

But a wedding ring wasn't needed as a symbol of this marriage. All the family and friends who were gathered together this day knew that Bob's life was changed forever the day he fell in love with a young woman named Mary who was wearing a red beret and sipping a soda at a drugstore counter.

Books You Can Read with Your Children

Somebody Loves You, Mr. Hatch
by Eileen Spinelli

All the Places to Love
by Patricia MacLachlan

Love You Forever
by Robert Munsch

Guess How Much I Love You
by Sam McBratney

I Love You, Little One
by Nancy Tafuri

Saint Valentine
by Robert Sabuda

Beauty and the Beast
Walt Disney (Book or Videotape)

Books and Resources for Parents

Don't You Really Love Me?
by Joseph M. Champlin

Courage to Love . . . When Your Marriage Hurts
by Gerald Foley

Once More With Love: A Guide to Marrying Again
by Bobbi Coyle-Hennessey

The Couple's Comfort Book
by Jennifer Louden

The Conscious Heart
by Kathlyn Hendricks, Ph.D., and Gay Hendricks, Ph.D.

Conversation Starters

1. Talk about a time this week when you felt loved by someone. How did it feel?

2. Can you think of a way that God shows you that he loves you?

Prayer

Loving God, sometimes it's impossible to imagine that you love us no matter how far we stray from you. Help us to bring some measure of that love into our families. When our words and actions hurt those whom we love, remind us of the need for forgiveness. Help us also to reach out with love and support to those who are struggling with broken marriages and carrying heavy burdens in their families. Hold us in your loving embrace and teach us to love our children the way you love each one of us. Amen.

The Third Week of February

Sick and Tired

It's 4:00 a.m. and my son, Bobby, is playing in the bath—an oatmeal bath. He has come down with the chicken pox and the bath seems to bring him relief. As the oatmeal bath works its magic, and once again Bobby is itch-free and happy, he begins playing with his Star Wars spaceships, imagining that the clumps of oatmeal surrounding him are exploding asteroids. I, on the other hand, am not as easily amused at this hour. I look and feel as if I've just stepped out of *The Night of the Living Dead* and it will be months before I make a batch of oatmeal cookies again.

This peculiar virus of spots and scabs brings contrasting responses from neighbors and friends. Since Bobby first came down with the chicken pox, friends are either heading for the hills or are urging us to invite them over during peak exposure time.

As I dab calamine lotion on Bobby and calculate the number of days until his sister, Teresa, breaks out, I realize how weary I've become with sickness these past few months. Because Bobby has had chronic ear infections and Teresa has asthma, sometimes even the common cold can make the kids miserable. New and more persistent flus and viruses are reported just as we've recovered from the previous illness. There are days when I'll go to great lengths to avoid these illnesses. My family could single-handedly keep the antibacterial soap companies in business. I'm not alone. I heard a collective sigh of relief when our associate pastor announced to his congregation of coughers one Sunday that we would refrain from offering each other a sign of Christ's peace.

As humidifiers hum and fevers flare, I realize how impatient I am with illness. Being sick or taking care of someone who's ill can be draining and

In God's Words

My child, when you are ill, do not delay, but pray to the Lord, and he will heal you.

— Sirach 38:9

Then give the physician his place, for the Lord created him; do not let him leave you, for you need him. There may come a time when recovery lies in the hands of physicians, for they too pray to the Lord that he grant them success in diagnosis and in healing, for the sake of preserving life.

— Sirach 38:12-14

Are any among you suffering? They should pray. . . . Are any among you sick? They should call for the elders of the church and have them pray over them, anointing them with oil in the name of the Lord. The prayer of faith will save the sick, and the Lord will raise them up; and anyone who has committed sins will be forgiven.

— James 5:13-15

What Can a Family Do?

1. In your daily prayers, include special intentions for those who are sick or suffering and those who care for them.

2. If you have family members or friends who are sick, talk about specific ways that you can help them, e.g., visit them in the hospital, send homemade get well cards and photos, make a dinner or dessert for the family, surprise them by doing some yard work, or offer to babysit.

3. Read the Gospel story of the Good Samaritan (Luke 10:25-37). How did the Samaritan treat the sick and injured man?

4. Read the miracles of Jesus healing the sick in the New Testament. Talk about why Jesus healed these men, women, and children. What was their response?

5. Learn more about the Sacrament of the Sick. How does it brings God's special blessing to those who are sick, suffering, or dying?

frustrating. We are in a weakened state, homebound, and taken away from our daily routine. The most difficult part is watching a loved one suffer, no matter how minor the illness.

Our popular culture is obsessed with physical fitness and good health as seen through daily advertisements, music videos, television programs, and movies. Sickness is often perceived as a sign of weakness. We may become uncomfortable when we're around people who are chronically ill or recovering from a serious illness or accident. They're a reminder that we too could be sick and suffering in ways far worse than a virus or flu. We feel compassion for them and their families, but after our dutiful visit we can close the door and walk away, relieved that we're not the one battling depression, suffering with cancer, or waiting for our child's medical test results.

What I've discovered in recent years is that we have much to learn from those who are sick and suffering. Rather than closing the door we should be opening our hearts. It's a privilege to sit and talk with people who are sick or suffering. When we reach out and really listen to them, seeing how they're meeting their crisis with faith, courage, and peace can deepen our faith. It also invites us to reflect on our lives and to make changes or realize what's truly important. I have friends who talk about their illness as a gift rather than a curse. A cancer survivor will talk about the important insights and perspectives he's gained rather than the days or months he's lost as a result of his illness. A victim of a senseless accident will tell you that she never realized the inner strength she had until the accident. And a parent whose faith was far off track has become close to God during his child's hospital stay. I'm not sure how this happens. But somehow through all the months of pain and heartbreak, we can grow personally and spiritually.

It's true that not everyone is able to use sickness as an opportunity for spiritual and personal growth. An elderly person may be too confused or frightened to understand his illness. Someone living with AIDS may have been ostracized by family members or coworkers and believes she's also been abandoned by God. Those who are mentally ill may be unable to face the reality of their illness.

I'm not convinced that "God never gives anyone a cross they're unable to bear." I know many good people who have been crushed by the crosses they've had to carry. We've all had our times when we too would be crushed under the weight of our crosses if not for the prayers and loving support of family, friends, and parishioners. Mother Teresa was fond of reminding us that we have a responsibility not only to reach out to those who are sick and suffering, but to unite with them in their suffering and bring them the love of Jesus. Even one caring person reaching out with this love can help a suffering person pick up his cross and know that Jesus walks beside him.

We certainly don't need to go looking for sorrow and sickness in order to deepen our relationship with God. And I don't believe that God causes bad things to happen to us. But God knows that just as blessings and joys come into our lives, so do sorrow and pain. When we experience life's tragedies and disappointments, God goes through the pain with us. We need to remember that Jesus experienced the tragedy and pain of the cross. When we cry out that our illness isn't fair or that the accident just doesn't make sense, we're reminded that the crucifixion is about as unfair and senseless as it gets. Like most people facing pain and suffering, Jesus pleaded with God to "let this cup pass from me." But by surrendering his will to His Father, his tragedy turned to triumph, bringing salvation to the world.

Two weeks after Bobby's first spot appeared, Teresa announced, "I'm very itchy and I have a hundred headaches." As I go through major and minor illnesses and accidents with my family, I hope I can keep in mind the words of St. Paul: "[God] consoles us in all our affliction, so that we may be able to console those who are in any affliction with the consolation with which we ourselves are consoled by God" (2 Corinthians 1:4).

Books You Can Read with Your Children

Little Brown Bear Is Sick
by Claude Lebrun

Henry and Mudge Get the Cold Shivers
by Cynthia Rylant

One Cow Coughs: A Counting Book for the Sick and Miserable
by Christine Loomis

When Vera Was Sick
by Vera Rosenberry

Tommy Catches a Cold (Rugrats Paperbacks)
by Sarah Wilson

I've Got Chicken Pox
by True Kelley

Germs Make Me Sick! (Let's Read and Find Out Science)
by Melvin Berger

When Molly Was in the Hospital: A Book for Brothers and Sisters of Hospitalized Children
by Debbie Duncan (Minimed Series)

Who's Sick Today?
by Lynne Cherry

Young People and Chronic Illness: True Stories, Help and Hope
by Kelly Huegel

Conversation Starters

1. Have you ever had a contagious illness—chicken pox, strep throat, a stomach virus? How did it feel knowing that you had to kept away from others so they wouldn't get sick? What helped you to feel better when you were sick?

2. How should we take care of the sick? How does Jesus ask us to care for the sick and suffering?

Prayer

Dear Jesus, our healer, thank you for the gift of good health. Too often, we take this gift for granted. We pray for those who are sick and those who care for them—at home, in hospitals, in nursing homes, and elsewhere. We pray for doctors, nurses, social workers, technicians, medical people, family, and friends who help to heal those who are sick and suffering. Give all those we know who are struggling with an illness comfort in your promise that you will one day turn all our sorrow into joy. Amen.

The Fourth Week of February

The Season of Lent

Silence Is Golden

Noise has always been a big part of my life. With four brothers and one sister, the sounds of silence were nowhere to be found in my family's home. The sounds of the television, radio, stereo, laughter, fighting, teasing, game playing, and lively conversations were the sounds I grew up with. "Stop that rough-housing!" was the one sound heard above all others.

During my school years, I found it difficult to do my homework without rock 'n' roll playing in the background. And somehow it didn't seem like a Saturday morning unless I woke up to the blare of a lawnmower's engine coming to life or the grunts of football players practicing their drills at our nearby high school.

Then I had my children. Nothing makes you crave silence and solitude more than a crying newborn. If you have an infant with colic (which we had) you may find yourself in a corner of the basement or an attic crawl space in your own fetal position pleading for fifteen minutes of peace and quiet.

Soon after parents have made it through their toddler's tears, the whining years begin. And you thought you craved silence when they were babies! My husband, Joe, who has an extraordinary amount of patience with our two children, has a tough time when it comes to whining. In exasperation one night he started "The Whiney Patrol," a group of invisible police whose mission it is to find the whiners and tickle them until they stop. It works. There's still a lot of noise in our house, but at least there's less whining.

We live in a world where we are bombarded by noise. We seem to be uncomfortable with quiet, stillness, or even a brief lull in the conversation. Rather than listening to the rhythms of our souls, we're

In God's Words

"Listen to me in silence, O coastlands; let the peoples renew their strength."

— Isaiah 41:1

Be silent before the Lord God! For the day of the Lord is at hand.

— Zephaniah 1:7

And after he had dismissed the crowds, he went up the mountain by himself to pray.

— Matthew 14:23

What Can a Family Do?

1. Ask your children to have "quiet time" each day.

2. Plant a garden with your family.

3. Take a hike through the woods and enjoy its peacefulness. Bring a picnic.

4. Visit a quiet place with your children—a church, a museum, a library.

caught up in the beat of television news, talk radio, video games, car phones, the daily newspaper, and the Internet. We're a society of achievers and doers, not meditators and reflectors. Our actions are often influenced by our outside world which hinders many opportunities to discover a world inside ourselves.

Most parents realize how necessary it is to find a few quiet moments each day and at the same time they recognize how nearly impossible this is to achieve. Throughout this season of Lent, we hear about the importance of listening, prayer, and silence. Just as in a conversation where we can only listen to what another person is saying if we are quiet, so too we can only open our minds and our hearts to what God is asking of us when we are still and silent.

I think we can give our children a wonderful gift if we build a little quiet time into their day. Ask your children to spend an hour in quiet time every afternoon—to read, to dream, to imagine, to be still, and to listen to their hearts. As a mother of two spirited children, I know this is easier said than done. On especially challenging days with my kids, I often take them to the library. A library is very appealing to me—a place where there is actually a rule to be quiet!

It's also important for parents to participate in quiet activities with their children: a hike in the woods, a trip to a museum, or a visit to church. Try to closely monitor the noise in your children's life by limiting the time spent watching television or playing video games. We need to let our children know that we value peace and quiet in the truest meanings of those words.

In a deeply spiritual work entitled *Dakota: A Spiritual Geography*, writer and poet Kathleen Norris reflects on her almost twenty years spent on the Dakota Plains. Ms. Norris is a married Protestant woman who has formed special relationships with the monks and nuns of the Benedictine communities in the Dakotas.

She writes, "Silence is the best response to mystery. . . . The silence of the plains, this great unpeopled landscape of earth and sky, is much like the silence one finds in a monastery, an unfathomable silence that has the power to reform you. . . . It was the Plains that first drew me to the monastery, which I suppose is ironic, for who would go seeking a desert within a desert? The irony and wonder of all this is that it is the desert's grimness, its stillness and isolation that bring us back to love. Here we discover the paradox of the contemplative life, that the desert of solitude can be the school where we learn to love others."

Silence isn't about isolation. It's a way to refresh and restore ourselves so we have the ability to know our true selves, to focus on what's really important and to discover ways that we can reach out to others. The quiet moments of our day can help us to appreciate God's handiwork in a beautiful sunset or a perfect spring day. And if we're really lucky, these silent times for prayer and reflection might even help us to see the presence of God in a whining child.

Books You Can Read with Your Children

The Quiet Noisy Book
by Margaret Wise Brown

Too Much Noise
by Ann McGovern

Night Noises
by Mem Fox

Noisy!
by Shirley Hughes

The Miracle Worker
by Jack M. Bickham (Book or Videotape)

The Very Quiet Cricket
by Eric Carle

Books and Resources for Parents

Dakota: A Spiritual Geography
by Kathleen Norris

Cloister Walk
by Kathleen Norris

From a Monastery Kitchen: The Classic Natural Foods Cookbook
by Brother Victor-Antoine d'Avila-Latourrette

The Seven Storey Mountain
by Thomas Merton

Care of the Soul
by Thomas Moore

Quiet Places with Jesus
by Isaias Powers

Quiet Places with Mary
by Isaias Powers

Out of Solitude
by Henri J. M. Nouwen

With Open Hands
by Henri J. M. Nouwen

Conversation Starters

1. Why do you think we need some "peace and quiet" in our lives? Can you think of one way that we can build this into our family life?

2. Why do you think Jesus went off by himself to pray sometimes?

Prayer

O Gracious God, in our busy and noisy lives, may we set aside a little quiet time each day to be with our families and with you. Help us to turn down the unnecessary noise in our lives. Let us listen to the quiet and gentle sounds of nature so that we can appreciate your marvelous creation. Help us to remember the importance of silent time for prayer and reflection—a time when we can listen to you and your word. We ask this through Christ our Lord. Amen.

The First Week of March

The ABCs of Lent

I love the month of March, perhaps because both of my children were born during this month. During March we mark the coming of spring and the beginning of Lent. It is a season of renewal and rebirth, a time of year when we set goals, clean house, and get busy. During Lent, we are also invited to get busy in our spiritual life by deepening our prayer and growing closer to God through serving the hungry, homeless, and heartbroken.

In the hectic hours of our busy days it seems that we hardly have time for those in our immediate family. How can we possibly find time to pray more or to reach out to a family in need whom we have never met? Yet, as Christian families, we are presented with the challenge of discovering Jesus in both the familiar families in our neighborhood and the forgotten families of our communities. This requires love, patience, and time, all of which are at a premium in our busy lives.

Still, there are many ways to begin teaching Christian service to our children that don't have to require a lot of our time, only a commitment to faith and love. The most important way we educate our children about our faith in God and service to others is by setting an example. There are many opportunities for practicing simple acts of kindness as a family that can help create in our children a profound awareness and sensitivity for people in need.

You may be already practicing some of the following suggestions in your home, but we need to remind ourselves and our children that these are all ways that we follow Jesus' invitation to "love one another." Here are twenty-six ideas—from A to Z—that family, friends, priests, sisters, and teachers have taught me in recent years:

In God's Words

"I was hungry and you gave me food, I was thirsty and you gave me something to drink, I was a stranger and you welcomed me, I was naked and you gave me clothing, I was sick and you took care of me, I was in prison and you visited me. . . . Truly I tell you, just as you did it to one of the least of these who are members of my family, you did it to me."

— Matthew 25:35-36, 40

Speak out for those who can not speak, for the rights of all the destitute. Speak out, judge righteously, defend the rights of the poor and needy.

— Proverbs 31:8-9

What Can a Family Do?

1. Do as many things as you can from A to Z in "The ABCs of Lent."

2. Add your own ideas to the list and share it with friends, so it continues to grow.

3. My seventeen-year-old niece, Nicole, recently participated in a program called "Locks of Love" when she had her hair cut. If you have eight inches or more of your hair cut off, you can donate it to "Locks of Love," who will use the hair to make wigs (at no cost) for children undergoing chemotherapy. Phone: 888-896-1588; website: www.locksoflove.com

Adopt a poor child in a mission program with every family member making a small contribution each month.

Bake a cake with your kids and share it with a neighbor.

Compliment your son or daughter when you notice they are sharing.

Donate food, clothing, furniture, or your time to an organization that serves the needy.

Encourage your children to use patience and fairness in resolving conflicts with their friends.

Fight against hatred and prejudice. Refuse to tolerate hateful attitudes, racial and ethnic jokes in your own family or anywhere else.

Give an hour each week to a family member or friend who is struggling with an addiction or raising a child alone. Visit with them, send a kind note, and pray for them.

Host a baby shower with your neighbors and donate the items to a local program for unwed mothers.

Invite a friend for dinner who has recently lost her job or suffered any kind of personal setback. Listen to her fears and explore ways that you may be able to assist her.

Jot a note, write a letter, or pick up the telephone to protest federal, state, or local legislation that undermines human life and dignity.

Kiss and hug your children often. Love begins at home.

Look for examples of racism, sexism, and violence when watching TV with your child and discuss them.

Make a meal for someone in need—a person ill with AIDS, a single mother or father, a friend who has lost a loved one.

Nurture your children's gifts of kindness, forgiveness, and love—celebrate the many ways they express them.

Offer to go food shopping for a neighbor or a parishioner who is recovering from an illness, or who is unable to leave her home.

Pray regularly as a family, especially for the needs of the poor, the lonely, and the oppressed.

Quit saying how you wish you had the time to volunteer and do something small. Talk to your children about your experience as a volunteer.

Read and discuss books with your children that emphasize compassion for others, such as a story of a saint or a champion of social justice.

Smile at your children when you see they are showing love and compassion to a grandparent, a neighbor, or friend.

Take your older children to a nursing home or soup kitchen. Hold hands with an elderly woman or a homeless man while you are there.

Use your talents to offer assistance in your parish, your child's school, the Special Olympics, or another worthy non-profit organization.

Volunteer as a family once a week, once a month, or once a year.

Welcome new neighbors of all cultures into your community and new parishioners into your church with joy and warmth.

Xerox an article which focuses on love, peace, or justice; send it to a family member, a friend, a priest, or teacher.

Yield not to society's pressures to buy excessive material things or violent toys, especially at Christmas and on birthdays. Explain your decision to your children.

Zap hatred wherever you find it and replace it with love.

Books You Can Read with Your Children

I Can Hear the Sun: A Modern Myth
by Patricia Polacco

Peppe the Lamplighter
by Elisa Bartone

Tico and the Golden Wings
by Leo Lionni

Stone Soup
by Marcia Brown

The Little Match Girl
by Hans Christian Anderson

A Song For Lena
by Hilary Horder Hippely

Rainbow Fish
by Marcus Pfister

A Crack in the Wall
by Mary Elizabeth Haggerty

Somebody Loves You, Mr. Hatch
by Eileen Spinelli

The Kid's Guide to Social Action
by Barbara A. Lewis
(Updated Edition)

The Kid's Guide to Service Projects: Over 500 Service Ideas for Young People Who Want to Make a Difference
by Barbara A. Lewis

Books and Resources for Parents

Heart of Joy: The Transforming Power of Self-Giving
by Mother Teresa

Les Misérables
by Victor Hugo

Parenting for Peace and Justice: Ten Years Later
by James and Kathleen McGinnis

Communities of Salt and Light: Reflections on the Social Mission of the Parish
by the National Conference of Catholic Bishops

Putting Children and Families First: A Challenge to Our Church and Nation
by the National Conference of Catholic Bishops

Conversation Starters

1. What do you like better—giving or receiving? Why?

2. Can you think of a time when you needed someone's help? How did it make you feel when someone was kind to you?

Prayer

Dear God, we hardly have time within our own families to be together, how can we possibly find the time to reach out to others in need of our help? But that's what you ask us to do. Guide us to make the right decisions when it comes to our priorities. When we struggle with the pressures of work and family, help us remember that every night far too many families wonder where will they sleep and what will they eat. Help us to bring your love and compassion to these forgotten families and all those we meet who need our help. We ask this through Christ our Lord. Amen.

The Second Week of March

Journey to the Kingdom

The guide books, maps, notebooks, and check lists were spread across our dining room table for weeks. During that time we gathered information on where to go, when to go, and how to get there. We had guide books from experts who had been there thirty-seven times and would give us "insider tips on how to see and do it all." We had dinner with friends who helped us plan our day-by-day itineraries and instructed us on how to avoid the pitfalls of first time visitors. Our countdown calendar hung in the kitchen and was closely followed with each passing day.

On the day of our departure, I whisked away our two children at their school dismissal. As we darted to our car, a neighbor yelled in our direction, "Where are you all going?" As if the cameras were rolling, the kids hollered back in unison, "We're going to Disney World!"

But as we waited to board our plane, our daughter, Teresa, who was six years old at the time, began to cough from the all the cigarette smoke in the crowded gate area. Once we got on the plane, we thought her coughing would subside, but it got worse. I had a pocket inhaler of Teresa's asthma medicine which I was sure would bring her relief. Instead, thirty minutes into the flight, her cough worsened. At an altitude of 35,000 feet, she patted my arm and calmly said, "I need a doctor because I'm having trouble breathing." All thoughts of our trip to the Magic Kingdom vanished and the only magic we wanted was for Teresa to be safe and healthy.

The announcement quickly came over the plane's intercom system: "If you have any medical training, please press your flight attendant button now." Minutes later, an internist from Lancaster, Pennsylvania, who was traveling to Disney World

In God's Words

"Do not be afraid, little flock, for it is your Father's good pleasure to give you the kingdom. . . . Make purses for yourselves that do not wear out, an unfailing treasure in heaven, where no thief comes near and no moth destroys. For where your treasure is, there your heart will be also."

— Luke 12:32-34

For the kingdom of God is not food and drink but righteousness and peace and joy in the Holy Spirit.

— Romans 14:17

Jesus answered, "My kingdom is not from this world."

— John 18:36

What Can a Family Do?

1. As a family, read about some of the Old Testament kings: Saul, David, and Solomon. What were their strengths and weaknesses?

2. Read the story of Jesus before Pilate (John 18). Why were the rulers and soldiers making fun of Jesus as a king? How did Jesus respond?

3. Read the Beatitudes (Matthew 5).What is Jesus saying about his kingdom?

with her seven-year-old son, was examining Teresa. The doctor reassured us that Teresa's condition wasn't life threatening but she was struggling and needed to get more medicine into her lungs. The doctor then constructed an aerochamber inhaler from an empty toilet paper roll so the medicine would be shot directly into Teresa's lungs.

During the rest of the flight, Teresa continued to cough, but was much improved. We never stopped praying and believed our prayers had been answered by this kind doctor and the caring passengers and crew aboard the plane. We were so relieved when we landed in Orlando and were greeted by Teresa's grandparents. The fresh Florida air and Disney World worked their magic on Teresa. During a house call from "Mickey Mouse's doctor," Teresa said, "Probably I was having trouble breathing on the plane because they didn't open the windows!"

We returned home from Disney World one week before Lent began, though in many ways it seemed that Lent had already begun. A few frightening moments on a plane with our daughter forced us to look inward and to reflect and pray about what was most important in our lives.

On Ash Wednesday, our pastor talked about the spiritual journey we would be taking over the next forty days. As we began our Lenten spiritual journey, the books, maps, checklists, and calendars that had cluttered our dining room table were gone. We were now on a journey to a very different kingdom. While I'm sure that God wants us to enjoy our recreational time with our families, Jesus' words remind us that we must "strive first for the kingdom of God" (Matthew 6:33).

The kingdom of God was the central theme of Jesus' preaching and parables. He invited everyone to enter this kingdom. It wasn't limited to the rich, the powerful, or the religious. Jesus lets us know too that the road to this kingdom is often paved with suffering, pain, doubt, and confusion. Throughout Lent we hear that suffering is the way to glory. It's difficult to listen to this message. We don't want to suffer; we'd rather go to Disney World. Yet many of us can say that the times we've truly grown in our faith are the times of great personal struggle and pain. Even knowing that, we certainly don't welcome pain into our lives. We prefer to focus on the resurrection rather than the passion.

The real magic in the kingdom of God is that our lifelong dreams for justice, peace, love, and life everlasting really can come true—if we seek this kingdom before everything else. St. Francis de Sales said it best: "Resolve henceforth to keep heaven before your mind, to be ready to forego everything that can hinder you or cause you to stray on your journey there."

Books You Can Read with Your Children

How Leo Learned to Be King
by Marcus Pfister

King Bob's New Clothes
by Dom DeLuise

The Children of the King
by Max Lucado

Arthur and the Sword
by Robert Sabuda

Disney's The Lion King
(Disney Classic Series)
by Don Ferguson

Kingdom Parables: Favorite Bible Parables for Children
by Christopher A. Lane

The Jewel Kingdom (Series)
by Jahnna N. Malcolm

The Barefoot Book of Princesses
retold by Caitlin Matthews

The Parables of Jesus
by Tomie dePaola

Books and Resources for Parents

Happy Are They: Living the Beatitudes in America
by Jim Langford

Conversation Starters

1. If you were king or queen, what kind of leader would you be? What would be the most important decision you would make for your kingdom?

2. What kind of king is God? What are the rules in his kingdom?

Prayer

Dear God, during this season of Lent, help us journey closer to you. Through prayer, reflection, and service to others, let us learn more about your kingdom. It's difficult to follow some of your spiritual teachings and so easy to become distracted with our material world. This Lent, help us to put you at the center of our lives. May we never forget that in your kingdom all are welcome and our dreams for peace, justice, love, forgiveness, and joy really can come true. But only if we seek your kingdom before everything else. Amen.

The Third Week of March

Interfaith Friendships

My husband, Joe, and I joined our children, Bobby and Teresa, to watch the *Rugrats' Passover Special*. When the program was over, Bobby asked, "Aren't we just a little bit Jewish, Mom?" I told Bobby that one of his uncles is Jewish and two of his cousins are Jewish, but he is Catholic. "I know I'm Catholic. But I really want to be Jewish too," he said.

Bobby's desire to be Jewish comes not only from the fact that his favorite cartoon program has Jewish characters—or that he can spin a mean dreidel—but also because he attends a public school where two of his close friends and his former kindergarten teacher are Jewish. During his school's winter sing-along, there were songs, stories, and poems about Christmas, Hanukkah, Las Posadas, and Kwanzaa. There were also Asian and Native American stories and songs, reflecting the wonderful diversity of religions and cultures of all the students.

I can't help but think how fortunate my children are to have this exposure to the traditions, customs, and beliefs of different cultures and religions. I know that most of today's Catholic schools have non-Catholic students and children of many cultures. While Catholic education is taught and Catholic values and beliefs permeate the school, there is a respect for other religious traditions and a celebration of diversity. And of course public schools can offer an even wider diversity.

I've heard it said on more than a few occasions that all this exposure can confuse a child or weaken their faith. It's too bad some people feel this way. Aren't we confident enough in our own faith to expose our children to what others believe? Do we lack knowledge of our religion or fail to live out our roles as teachers of the faith? Do our children see

In God's Words

"I ask not only on behalf of these, but also on behalf of those who will believe in me through their word, that they may all be one."

— John 17:20

"Above all, clothe yourselves with love, which binds everything together in perfect harmony."

— Colossians 3:14

What Can a Family Do?

1. Teach your children all about their faith through your word and example. Be open to their questions and comments about other religions.

2. Teach your children to learn about other religions and the impact that religion has always had in world history and politics. If you don't know the answers to their questions, go to the library, get on the Internet, or better yet, ask a friend of a different faith.

3. Take your family to interfaith prayer services, concerts, or other events.

that our faith is at the center of who we are and what we're about? When children have a strong understanding of their faith, there's a good chance they will be curious about other faiths.

We live in a world where people have been persecuted and wars have been waged over religious hatred and intolerance. When I read about another bomb being set off in the Middle East or Northern Ireland, I find my son's interest in other religions refreshing and hopeful. We have a ways to go when it comes to speaking out whenever our religion is being attacked or unfairly depicted in the media or by others. But we also have an enormous responsibility to teach our children to love and respect people of other religious traditions and to gather with other Christians united in the bond of Jesus. I love my Church and believe her teachings with all my heart, but I know many people of other faiths who love God and their church as deeply as I love mine.

Seven years ago I became friends with Fran, a woman in my neighborhood and the mother of three children who happens to be Protestant. We discovered how important faith was to both of us and to our families. For the first time, I experienced a friendship that was founded on faith. Over the years, we shared so much about our different faiths and the misconceptions we had about each other's religion. Fran's prayers and words of God's love helped me through some of my most difficult hours. Her unshakable faith and knowledge of the Bible have deeply enriched my spiritual life.

Over the years we've talked at our kitchen tables, in hospital rooms, on the beach, or over the phone. I've often felt that God was smiling on us, pleased that we transcended the stereotypes and instead focused on what united us. I am a better Catholic because of Fran's love and example.

For me, having a friend who is Catholic is a bit like putting on a pair of old shoes. They're comfortable. They feel right. We've walked on familiar and common ground together. Meeting a friend who isn't Catholic may be more like buying a pair of new shoes. At first they might be uncomfortable; they may be a style or color that we normally wouldn't buy; we're unsure how they'll look on us. I believe God is telling us we need to wear both kinds of shoes on our journey of faith. We need the loving and mutual support of our family of faith—its beliefs, traditions, and values we have known and loved for years. But we also need the richness of other religions and cultures that reflect the diversity of the world God created.

The most effective way we can work toward the unity that God wishes for all the world's people is to be a shining example of God's love in the way we treat all people rather than claiming religious superiority. And one of the first places we begin this is by teaching our own "Rugrats" through word and example to be respectful of the many ways people search for God in our world.

Books You Can Read with Your Children

My Friends' Beliefs—A Young Reader's Guide to World Religions
by Hiley H. Ward

Children Just Like Me—A Unique Celebration of Children Around the World
by Barnabas and Anabel Kindersley

Celebrations Around the World: A Multicultural Handbook
by Carole S. Angell

The Christmas Menorahs: How a Town Fought Hate
by Janice Cohn, DSW

Conversation Starters

1. What would a world be like to you if everything was the same?

2. Do you have friends of different religions? Have you talked to each other about what makes your religions special?

Prayer

God, Creator of all people, we live in a world where there is great religious and cultural diversity. Help us to see how our differences can enrich us. We thank you for the special relationship we have with our Jewish sisters and brothers. And we are grateful for the faith of other Christians, with whom we share so many beliefs. Help us to respect the many ways people search for you. May we work and pray for a better understanding of all religions. Amen.

The Fourth Week of March

"Was Jesus Ever Put in 'Time Out'?"

It was a particularly challenging Monday afternoon. My son, Bobby, who was two-and-a-half years old at the time, was on his way to the "time out" chair for the third time in less than twenty minutes for chasing our dog Whisper with a soup ladle. A few minutes later, while I was taking my own time out, I found myself wondering what Mary might have done on the days when Jesus was a handful.

Did Mary ever put Jesus in time out? Did Joseph build a chair specifically for this purpose? What would Mary do if Jesus refused to eat what she prepared for supper? What tactics did Joseph resort to on the days that Jesus decided he didn't want to wear his coat? Did Mary and Joseph ever suffer from sleep deprivation because Jesus climbed into their bed at night and kicked them in his sleep all night long? Because Jesus was both fully human and divine, he had to have gone through the "terrible twos." How did they cope?

There is surprisingly little recorded about the life of Jesus as a child. What was Jesus like as a boy? What were Mary and Joseph like as parents? I can only imagine how meaningful and helpful it would be for parents everywhere to read Mary's and Joseph's reflections on the joys and challenges of parenthood.

Through the Gospels of Luke and Matthew, we know that Jesus came into this world as a baby with a loving mother and father at his side. We also know that Jesus, Mary, and Joseph fled to Egypt when they learned that Herod was searching for the child Jesus to destroy him. After Herod's death the Holy Family settled in Nazareth where they lived until Jesus began his public ministry around the age of thirty.

In God's Words

God is treating you as children; for what child is there whom a parent does not discipline? Moreover, we had human parents to discipline us, and we respected them. Should we not be even more willing to be subject to the Father of spirits and live? For they disciplined us for a short time as seemed best to them, but he disciplines us for our good, in order that we may share his holiness.

— Hebrews 12:7, 9-10

Children, obey your parents in the Lord, for this is right. "Honor your father and mother"—this is the first commandment with a promise: "so that it may be well with you and you may live long on the earth." And, fathers, do not provoke your children to anger, but bring them up in the discipline and instruction of the Lord.

— Ephesians 6:1-4

What Can a Family Do?

The following suggestions come from one of my favorite parenting experts, Marguerite Kelly. Her book, *Marguerite Kelly's Family Almanac*, (Doubleday) is a great resource for parents.

1. "Preventive discipline, like preventive medicine, stops most problems before they start. Children behave much better when most of their calories—even their snacks—are nutritious; when they get plenty of sleep at night; and when the pace at home is slow and there is time for them to talk and especially for you to listen."

2. "If your child is upset, he'll listen to you better if you let him explain his side first, and if you don't use the same old cliches. And if he's wailing? You'll get a softer answer if you use a softer voice or if you whisper and hug him while you talk."

3. "Whether you're dealing with homework or chores, you'll have much more luck if you inspect your child's work as soon as it's done and praise it whenever you can. Notice successes more than errors."

4. "You shouldn't be sarcastic or make comparisons between one child and another or say anything that starts with 'you,' because that's sure to be a negative statement and a personal one, and no one responds well to that."

5. "And of course, don't make global threats that you can't keep: 'If you don't behave you'll never watch TV again.'"

What about all those years in between? Any new parent is overwhelmed with the responsibilities that come with bringing a child into the world. How did Mary feel? St. Luke writes that following the visit of the shepherds to the simple stable in Bethlehem, "Mary treasured all these words and pondered them in her heart" (2:19).

I imagine that not only did Mary treasure all the things that she experienced as the Mother of God, but also those things she felt as the mother of a growing child. She must have cherished Jesus' first smile and the appearance of his first tooth. She must have often reflected on how fast her little boy was growing. Etched in her heart forever were all the times, but especially the first, when Jesus said, "I love you." And for all eternity she will never forget the joy she experienced with Jesus' first steps as a toddler and the heartache she endured watching his final steps on the road to Calvary.

The New Testament tells us only one story of Jesus as a boy, but I believe it provides all mothers and fathers with a great deal of strength, insight, and reassurance in their role as parents.

When Jesus was twelve, he went to the Temple with his parents to celebrate the feast of Passover. When the celebration was over, Mary and Joseph realized that Jesus was lost. They spent the next three days searching for him.

St. Luke writes: "When his parents saw him they were astonished, and his mother said to him: 'Child, why have you treated us like this? Look, your father and I have been searching for you in great anxiety.' He said to them, 'Why were you searching for me? Did you not know that I must be in my Father's house?'" (2:48-49).

Any parent whose son or daughter has been out of sight for three minutes, let alone three days, understands the worry and fear that Mary and Joseph were experiencing while looking for their lost child. And it is a bit comforting to know that even Mary used the line, "How could you do this to us?"

It sounds to me like Jesus was quite an independent and precocious child. I wonder if it was difficult for Mary to let go of Jesus as he went about his Father's business. She had to let go of her son sooner than most mothers do. I imagine that Mary and Joseph would have some reassuring words to say to parents of independent teenagers as well.

As young parents, how did Mary and Joseph feel knowing that the child they were responsible for raising was God's Son? (We think we feel pressure as parents!) The boy with whom they played during the day and whom they tucked in at night was the Son of God. The child who came into their lives in a simple stable became the turning point in human history. Jesus was God's Son who came to heal us, to save us, to free us, and to teach us how to live.

As the child Jesus grew into a man, He gave us the extraordinary gift of his words and actions to guide all of us on our journeys of faith. But Jesus' greatest gift, giving his life so that we could have the promise of eternal life, was also his mother's greatest sorrow. I believe that any parent who has lost a child at any age or has seen their child as a victim of hatred, prejudice, and injustice, understands to some degree the anguish and grief that Mary experienced as she stood at the foot of the cross watching Jesus die. For even though she knew it was the fulfillment of scripture, up on that cross was the Son of God, her son, and, at one time, her little boy.

What Can a Family Do?
(continued)

6. "Don't demand global promises that he can't keep. You'll just set him up for failure if you say, 'Promise me you'll never make fun of your sister again,' because he is going to make fun of her and he'll probably do it before the day is done. You're only trying to make him be a little kinder and a little quieter."

7. "You'll occasionally win the same Rotten Parent Award that all of us have won—the one that makes you apologize afterward and then keeps you awake for hours. . . . It teaches you one of life's greatest lessons: you can't expect perfection unless you're perfect too."

Books You Can Read with Your Children

Pierre
by Maurice Sendak

Where the Wild Things Are
by Maurice Sendak

Alexander and the Terrible, Horrible, No Good, Very Bad Day
by Judith Viorst

Eloise
by Kay Thompson

Curious George
by H. A. Rey

The Elephant and the Bad Baby
by Elfrida Vipont

The Tale of Peter Rabbit
by Beatrix Potter

Two Bad Ants
by Chris Van Allsburg

Can You Find Jesus?
by Philip Gallery

Jesus Grows Up
by Pilar Paris, Joseph Lozano, and Maria Rius

Books and Resources for Parents

Marguerite Kelly's Family Almanac
by Marguerite Kelly

Liberated Parents, Liberated Children: Your Guide to a Happier Family
by Adele Faber and Elaine Mazlish

How to Talk So Kids Will Listen and Listen So Kids Will Talk
by Adele Faber and Elaine Mazlish

The Seven Secrets of Successful Parents
by Randy Rolfe

Wonderful Ways to Love a Child
by Judy Ford

Wonderful Ways to Love a Teen . . . Even When It Seems Impossible
by Judy Ford

Children Learn What They Live: Parenting to Inspire Values
by Dorothy Law Nolte and Rachel Harris

Conversation Starters

1. Do you think Jesus was ever put in "time out"?

2. Do you know the difference between human and divine? Why do you think Jesus became human?

Prayer

Some days, we sit and wonder: What was my life like before my children came? What did I do with all my time? What was it like to finish a conversation in a normal time frame—without all the interruptions? The job of parent is like no other. No books, no parenting classes can ever prepare a first time parent for all they will experience and feel. It helps to know that Mary and Joseph experienced many of the same feelings that today's parents have felt.

Please be with us Lord as we navigate our way through this uncharted territory of parenthood. Help us not to take ourselves too seriously. May we try not to be too hard on our children or too hard on ourselves. We ask this through Christ our Lord. Amen.

The First Week of April

April 1 is April Fool's Day.

The Happy News

Last fall my husband's grandmother died at the age of 86. When Joe was a toddler he couldn't pronounce "Grandma Marie," so his beloved grandmother was forever dubbed "GiGi." Our children had the wonderful opportunity to get to know and love their great-grandmother. On the morning of GiGi's death, Joe told the kids he had some "very sad news, but also some happy news" that he wanted to share with them.

Joe said to Bobby and Teresa: "GiGi died this morning and I'm very sad because I loved her and I'm going to miss her so much. But now she's in heaven and all her suffering is over because she is with God." After a few moments of silence, Teresa looked up at her father and said, "And what's the happy news?"

During this Easter season we are all invited to celebrate the happy news of Jesus' resurrection. Through Jesus' triumph over death, each one of us who believes is promised the gift of eternal life. Easter is a feast of joy that can stay with us forever.

We're able to experience a greater joy of Easter because we've made the Lenten journey through the sorrow of our Lord's Passion. In our own lives, we often feel joy on a much deeper level after we've been through heartache, adversity, and suffering. Our challenge is to bring the joy of knowing and loving God into our hearts and the hearts of others, even as the crosses and cruelties of life come our way.

My good friend Dr. Barron Maberry, pastor of St. Matthew's Lutheran Church in Washington, D.C., has been conducting workshops on the healing power of laughter and humor for more than fifteen years. His most popular workshop, "Take Two Laughs and Call Me in the Morning," addresses

In God's Words

For everything there is a season, and a time for every matter under heaven . . . a time to weep, and a time to laugh.

— Ecclesiastes 3:1, 4

Make a joyful noise to the Lord, all the earth. Worship the Lord with gladness; come into his presence with singing.

— Psalm 100:1-2

Then our mouth was filled with laughter, and our tongue with shouts of joy; then it was said among the nations, "The Lord has done great things for them."

— Psalm 126:2

What Can a Family Do?

1. Whenever possible, talk about the joy found in our faith.

2. Read the story of Zacchaeus (Luke 19:1-10). Ask your children if there is humor in this story.

3. As a family, celebrate the joy of laughter by renting funny videos, telling jokes, and being silly.

4. In difficult situations, try to find humor whenever possible.

5. Teach your children that a good joke or humorous story should never be at the expense of hurting another person's feelings.

6. When your children get older, teach them the Joyful Mysteries of the Rosary and talk about why they're joyful: The Annunciation, The Visitation, The Birth of the Child Jesus, the Presentation in the Temple, and The Finding of the Child Jesus in the Temple.

humor as a positive spirit for us emotionally, physically, and spiritually.

On most days, the gifts of joy and laughter fill our world so completely that we take them for granted rather than seeing them as one of our greatest blessings. A baby's smile, a child's irrepressible laugh, or a case of the giggles can easily turn a dark mood into a playful one. Imagine what our world would be like if God hadn't given us the gift of laughter.

Dr. Maberry says that there are many benefits to spreading laughter and having a positive spirit: it stimulates our thinking, creates a positive mental and emotional state, produces endorphins to combat depression and anxiety, recaptures the gift of play, and helps us to live healthier and longer. He says: "We can give ourselves and others the gift of laughter and a positive spirit when we focus, meditate, and say the prayer, 'Good morning, God!' rather than, 'Good God, morning!' Most of all, laughter helps us not to take life and ourselves too seriously."

There are times when we all tend to take our religion too seriously. We forget that the words joy, rejoice, and happiness fill the Bible. After the birth of Jesus, the angels declared to the shepherds: "I am bringing you good news of great joy for all the people" (Luke 2:10). Jesus worked his first miracle during the joyous occasion of a wedding. Jesus' parables were about the joy of forgiveness. His miracles of healing brought hope and happiness to broken and desperate people. His Sermon on the Mount teaches us the way to find true happiness. During a prayer for the disciples on the night before he died, Jesus said, "So you have pain now; but I will see you again, and your hearts will rejoice, and no one will take your joy from you" (John 16:22).

Sometimes we leave the joy out of our religion because we don't see Jesus as a man who smiled, laughed, or enjoyed his disciples' jokes. My friend, Maria, has a charcoal drawing of a laughing Christ hanging in her living room. It has such a warm and comforting effect on all who see it because it shows a side of Jesus many of us have seldom seen. Why is it so hard to imagine a joyful Jesus? After all, Jesus was a passionate man full of all our human emotions, including joy. I find it difficult to believe that vast crowds of people would have followed him if he was humorless and gloomy. And anyone who has children knows that they would not have run into the arms of a man who was without joy and laughter in his heart.

Because we are made in the image and likeness of God, we know our God is a God of laughter as well as love. He longs for us to be joyful even in our sorrows and difficulties. The Holy Father has said, "In a true sense, joy is the keynote of the Christian message. With St. Paul I exhort you: 'Rejoice in the Lord always, I say it again, rejoice.' Rejoice because Jesus has come into the world! Rejoice because Jesus has died upon the cross! Rejoice because he rose from the dead! Rejoice because in baptism he washed way our sins! Rejoice because Jesus has come to set us free! And rejoice because he is the Master of our life!"

And that indeed, is the happy news!

Books You Can Read with Your Children

The Jester Has Lost His Jingle
by David Saltzman

The Stinky Cheese Man and Other Fairly Stupid Tales
by Jon Scieszka

The Little Giant Book of Jokes
by Joseph Rosenbloom

The Little Giant Book of Riddles
by Joseph Rosenbloom

The Little Giant Book of Knock Knocks
by Charles Keller

Laughing Together: Giggles and Grins from Around the Globe
by Barbara K. Walker

The Funny Little Woman
by Arlene Mosel

Books and Resources for Parents

The Joyful Christ
by Cal Samra. An uplifting book about an ecumenical grassroots movement called the Fellowship of Merry Christians, who seek to recapture the spirit, joy, humor, unity, and healing power of the early Christians. The fellowship publishes a newsletter, *The Joyful Noiseletter*, whose masthead carries a drawing of Christ laughing. For more information: P.O. Box 668, Kalamazoo, Michigan 49005.

Conversation Starters

1. Do you have a family member or friend who you think is funny? Why are they funny?

2. Do you think Jesus enjoyed laughter and humor? How do you know?

Prayer

Dear Lord, when we imagine a world without laughter, we realize what a magnificent gift you have given us. Thank you for all the laughter, jokes, and funny situations that bring so much joy into our lives. May we never take this gift for granted. Help us to look at the funny side of life. We know through your parables and stories that you had a good sense of humor. You used humor and joy to help people better understand the love God has for each one of us and how he longs for us to be happy. May our homes be filled with laughter and may we spread the joy of our faith to all those we meet. Amen.

The Second Week of April

A Place for Peace

The award is displayed prominently on our refrigerator and, although my son was only six at the time he received it, I can't imagine any other recognition he'll receive in the years ahead that will make my husband and me prouder than this one. The citation reads: "Bobby Marx has been named 'Peacemaker of the Week.' Acts of kindness, cleaning up, being helpful, thoughtful, and kind, and generally acting in a way that promotes peace in our class are some of the actions required to be honored in this way."

This award is part of the school's ongoing efforts to promote peace-making while always emphasizing that "Peace must first begin with me." The school also created a peace garden in one of the classrooms. Creations by the entire student body included two-foot-high sunflowers, bright blue crepe paper waterfalls and skies, a wall of butterflies declaring, "We Are Peace Seekers," and another wall of students' Poems For Peace. It's very clear from this exhibit that children have much to teach us about the true meaning of peace and how to achieve it.

But how do we talk to our children about peace? The most effective way we can teach children about peace is through our actions—forgiving easily, speaking kindly, praying for peace as a family, and speaking out against hatred and injustice. But with all the pressures of today's family life, it becomes a real challenge to set examples of peacemaking in our homes, especially when our communities and our world are touched by unspeakable acts of hatred and violence.

On April 19, as our nation commemorates the anniversary of the bombing of the Alfred P. Murrah Building in Oklahoma City, we are reminded that

In God's Words

"Blessed are the peacemakers, for they will be called children of God."

— Matthew 5:9

"Peace I leave with you; my peace I give to you."

— John 14:27

"Let them turn away from evil and do good; let them seek peace and pursue it."

— 1 Peter 3:11

What Can a Family Do?

1. Pray for peace as a family. Speak out against hatred and injustice.

2. Set examples of kindness and peacemaking in our own families; teach children to solve arguments with words, not fists.

3. When there is an argument in your home or with friends, emphasize the importance of forgiving one another.

4. Read Jesus' words about forgiveness with your children. Talk with them about what real forgiveness means—sometimes it's a difficult and painful process rather than a simple phrase.

5. Ask your children if they know what Jesus meant when he said we must forgive seventy times seven. How much is seventy times seven? Ask them to collect 490 pennies to show how much Jesus wants us to forgive one another. Should we stop at 490 times?

thousands of people in that community are struggling to let go of their anger and bitterness and are trying to find their way back to forgiveness and peace. The rest of us can only imagine how difficult it must be for the parents in Oklahoma City to teach their children about peace, justice, forgiveness, and hope in the midst of such personal tragedy and terror.

My family had a special interest as we listened to the first news reports from Oklahoma City on the day of the bombing. My brother, Brian, his wife, Rose, and their six children live in Edmond, Oklahoma, just fifteen miles north of Oklahoma City. Brian is a navy pilot at Tinker Air Force Base, eight miles east of the city. Because of the training Brian had received in his job, he knew instantly on that April morning that the sound that would forever shatter the lives of so many Oklahomans was a bomb. Their older children were at school as the bomb exploded. Six-year-old Katy was in her school library and, as she heard the explosion and felt the ground shake, she ran back to her classroom terrified that they were experiencing an earthquake. Rose was getting two of their younger children ready for nursery school when she felt the explosion. Because of the proximity to the Air Force base, she thought it might be a sonic boom. But as she turned on her car radio she heard hysterical screaming and frantic cries of "We need help. . . ."

Brian and Rose knew people who were killed and injured in the explosion. Seven people from their parish, St. John the Baptist in Edmond, were also killed. A year after the bombing, the parish dedicated its own peace garden as a memorial to those who died in the explosion. The stone slab listing the names of those parishioners killed will rest in the garden and is an actual piece of the Murrah Building.

Brian and Rose brought their children to the site of the bombing two weeks after the explosion at the request of their oldest son, Kevin, who was eleven at the time. Two weeks before the Murrah Building was imploded, Rose and her friend Jodie returned to the site again. "The TV coverage of the devastation was horrifying to watch but it's very different to be there in person and actually feel the broken glass under your feet," Rose said.

She continued, "At one point, Jodie and I wondered if we were being good mothers by taking our two youngest children downtown and looking at all the destruction. And then, as we came around a corner Jodie grabbed my arm and we saw something I will never forget. On the side of one of the buildings hit by the blast, an artist had painted a picture of the Murrah building. But instead of painting clouds of smoke from the explosion, the artist painted clouds in the shapes of angels. The angels represented some of the victims of the bombing and they were holding hands as they walked toward heaven. Jodie and I couldn't speak. We knew we were standing on sacred ground.

"The artist gave us a gift. It was a reminder that I want to teach my children that peace and love are stronger than violence and hatred. And that even though there are some people who do terrible things, most people are good and kind. Too many lives were destroyed and those people's lives will never be the same. But I believe that those men, women, and children who were killed so violently are now at peace, resting in God's loving hands."

Books You Can Read with Your Children

The Big Book For Peace
by Ann Durell

Dia's Story Cloth: The Hmong People's Journey of Freedom
by Dia Cha

One April Morning: Children Remember the Oklahoma City Bombing
by Nancy Lamb

Kids' Random Acts of Kindness
by the Conari Press Editors

Peaceful Kingdom: Random Acts of Kindness by Animals
by Stephanie Laland

Yertle the Turtle and Other Stories
by Dr. Seuss

The Wall
by Eve Bunting

Sadako and the Thousand Paper Cranes
by Eleanor Coerr

Books and Resources for Parents

Their Faith Has Touched Us: The Legacies of Three Young Oklahoma City Bombing Victims
by Maria Scarperlanda

Peacemaking: Moral and Policy Challenges for a New World
edited by Gerard F. Powers, Drew Christiansen, S.J., and Robert T. Hennemeyer

The Challenge of Peace: God's Promise and Our Response
by the National Conference of Catholic Bishops

Confronting a Culture of Violence
by the National Conference of Catholic Bishops (English and Spanish available)

Parenting for Peace and Justice: Ten Years Later
by Mitch and Kathleen Finley

Win the Whining War and Other Skirmishes: A Family Peace Plan
by Cynthia Whitham, MSW

Bound to Forgive: The Pilgrimage to Reconciliation of a Beirut Hostage
by Lawrence Martin Jenco, OSM

Return of the Prodigal Son
by Henri J.M. Nouwen

Prayer

Prayer of St. Francis

Lord, make me an instrument of your peace.
Where there is hatred, let me sow love;
where there is injury, pardon;
where there is doubt, faith;
where there is despair, hope;
where there is darkness, light;
and where there is sadness, joy.
O Divine Master, grant that I may not so much seek
to be consoled, as to console,
to be understood, as to understand,
to be loved, as to love.
For it is in giving that we receive;
in pardoning that we are pardoned;
and in dying that we are born to eternal life. Amen.

The Third Week of April

In April we celebrate Earth Day.

People and the Planet

"What are humans?" my son, Bobby, asked me one day when he was about four years old. "Humans? Oh, that's just another word for people," I told him. "Well, then, why are *humans* destroying the earth?" he demanded to know.

I wondered where this latest line of questioning was coming from. Then I remembered that a few days before, he had watched an animated movie at his cousin Patty's house called *Once Upon a Forest*. In the movie, three friends, Abigail the wood mouse, Edgar the mole, and Russell the hedgehog find their peaceful lives greatly disrupted by humans. A chemical spill has destroyed Dapplewood and their young friend Michelle has become seriously ill from the toxic fumes. The three friends race against time and the yellow dragons (bulldozers) to save Michelle.

At the age of four, Bobby was on a mission to keep the earth clean. One day, while we were at the park, I heard Bobby call out, "Moooommm." I wondered what rare discovery he had stumbled upon this time. Instead, he pointed to a crumpled-up candy wrapper on the ground and said with great disgust, "Littering!" Another of his environmental concerns was graffiti. In fact we had been discussing it and pointing it out so often that Bobby's sister, Teresa, who was two at the time, would yell out "GRAFFITI" each time we passed by the large, looped spray-painted letters.

As I listened to and watched my friends' children, it was easy to see that Bobby was not the only member of the recycling police. Many children lecture their parents about the importance of saving water and recycling glass and aluminum. These little enforcers of the environment already seemed to understand that when someone does something to

In God's Words

In the beginning when God created the heavens and the earth, the earth was a formless void and darkness covered the face of the deep, while a wind from God swept over the face of the waters. Then God said, "Let there be light"; and there was light.

— Genesis 1:1-3

O Lord, how manifold are your works! In wisdom you have made them all; the earth is full of your creatures.

— Psalm 104:24

You visit the earth and water it, you greatly enrich it; the river of God is full of water; you provide the people with grain, for so you have prepared it.

— Psalm 65:9

What Can a Family Do?

1. Recycle newspapers, glass, and aluminum.

2. Don't leave water running when brushing your teeth, washing your car, or shaving.

3. Fix leaky pipes, tune up your furnace, and lower your thermostat.

4. Join a "Clean Up Your Park Day."

5. Read the story of Creation to your children.

6. Read *The Circle of Days* by Reeve Lindbergh. It is based on "Canticle of the Sun," written by St. Francis of Assisi, a saint who loved nature and animals.

hurt the earth, it also hurts the people who inhabit the earth.

I care deeply about saving our planet, and my husband, Joe, and I do all we can to respect the environment. But I must confess we have not always been our children's primary educators on the environment. From the time Bobby and Teresa began watching TV, they listened to singing and dancing water droplets on Sesame Street ask, "Are You a Waster-ooo?" In our car we have listened to the well known children's entertainer Raffi sing out, "It's a big beautiful planet in the sky; the earth's our home, it's where we live." And in a popular touring stage production, "The Great Dinosaur Mystery," the song, "Extinction Stinks" is the favorite of all the environmentally correct songs.

In recent years, there has been a growing movement by actors, musicians, politicians, and concerned citizens to educate and advocate on behalf of the earth. Just last year, there was an artist-in-residence program about the Rain Forest at Bobby's and Teresa's elementary school. For two weeks, artists, dancers, and musicians taught the children about the importance of saving the Rain Forest. During the final day of the program, the school's gym was transformed into a Rain Forest with hand-made trees, red-eyed tree frogs, spider monkeys, anacondas, macaws, and butterflies. It was clear to us and many other parents that our children had much to teach us about saving the Rain Forest for future generations.

Our children have also taught us that the way we can change attitudes and practices is to teach these important lessons right from the start and to reinforce these messages throughout their lives. Although the work is far from complete, we now have a younger generation who have been raised with a respect for the earth and its resources.

This Earth Day, as we reflect on the many ways we can protect our planet, it's crucial for us to remember that God not only asks us to love the earth, he also asks to "love one another." Almost ten years ago, the bishops of the United States issued an important pastoral reflection, *Renewing the Earth: An*

Invitation to Reflection and Action on Environment in Light of Catholic Social Teaching. The bishops explored the links between concern for the person and concern for the earth. The bishops wrote, "The whole human race suffers as a result of environmental blight, and generations yet unborn will bear the cost for our failure to act today. But in most countries today, including our own, it is the poor and the powerless who most directly bear the burden of current environmental carelessness. Their lands and neighborhoods are more likely to be polluted or to host toxic waste dumps, their water to be undrinkable, their children to be harmed."

At the end of *Once Upon A Forest*, Michelle is rescued, thanks to the heroic efforts of her friends. As Michelle's teacher, Cornelius, surveys the damage from the chemical spill, he tells Michelle that if everyone works as hard to save Dapplewood as her friends worked to save her, their land won't be destroyed. We too must work together at building a world where we are committed to protecting our people and our planet.

Books You Can Read with Your Children

The Lorax
by Dr. Seuss

Old Turtle
by Douglas Wood

Once There Was a Tree
by Natalia Romanova

The Circle of Days
by Reeve Lindbergh

While a Tree Was Growing
by Jane Bosveld

When the Wind Stops
by Charlotte Zolotow

The Wind and the Willows
by Kenneth Grahame

Under the Sun and the Moon and Other Poems
by Margaret Wise Brown

Wonderful Earth!
by Nick Butterworth and Mick Inkpen

Pearl Moscowitz's Last Stand
by Arthur A. Levine

Books and Resources for Parents

Sharing Nature with Children
by Joseph Cornell

The Sense of Wonder
by Rachel Carson

Renewing the Earth: An Invitation to Reflection and Action on Environment in Light of Catholic Social Teaching
by the United States Bishops (To order call: 1-800-235-8722)

Conversation Starters

1. What can we do today to help to protect the earth?

2. Why does God want us to protect the earth?

Prayer

St. Francis' Canticle of the Sun
(Selected verses)

Praised be my Lord with all creatures;
and especially our brother the sun,
which brings us the day and the light;
fair is he, and shining with a very great
*   splendor:*
O Lord, he signifies you to us!

Praised be my Lord for our sister the
*   moon, and for the stars,*
which God has set clear and lovely in
*   heaven.*

Praised be my Lord for our brother the
*   wind,*
and for air and cloud, calms and all
*   weather,*
by which you uphold in life all creatures.

Praised be my Lord for our sister water,
which is very serviceable to us,
and humble, and precious, and clean.

Praised be my Lord for brother fire,
through which you give us light in the
*   darkness;*
and he is bright, and pleasant, and very
*   mighty, and strong.*

Praised be my Lord for our mother the
*   Earth,*
which sustains us and keep us,
and yields diverse fruits, and flowers of
*   many colors, and grass. Amen.*

The Fourth Week of April

"Take Our Daughters to Work Day" is celebrated at the end of April.

The Gift of Girls

My young daughter, Teresa, confidently grabs the orange rings hanging by the chains at her school playground. As she pauses on each ring, she gathers her momentum to seize the next ring. Her body swings rhythmically back and forth like a metronome, keeping the beat of a girl on the go. With grace and flare she easily leaps to the wooden platform and raises her arms in triumph like an Olympic gymnast. Teresa proudly turns my way and says, "Don't forget to clap, Mom." Her strength, agility, and confidence are a joy to behold.

On the opposite end of the playground, Teresa's older brother, Bobby, and his friends have finished a game of touch football. As the boys pass by Teresa, one of them makes an unkind remark to her. But with a broad smile and unflinching determination, she has no trouble putting this bothersome boy in his place. "Oh yeah. Well you're not bothering me. And I'm not listening to you, and I bet you can't skip the rings like I can." Although rebuked, the boy smiles at the moxie of his friend's little sister. I'm enjoying this moment as much as Teresa's success on the orange rings.

I'm taking in both these scenes with a new perspective because I've recently finished reading two eye-opening books about the daily dangers of being young and female in today's world: *Reviving Ophelia: Saving the Selves of Adolescent Girls* by Mary Pipher, Ph.D., and *The Body Project: An Intimate History of American Girls* by Joan Jacobs Brumberg. Both books take a serious look into the ways that our "look obsessed," "media saturated" culture oppresses girls and can ultimately destroy their sense of self. Despite all the gains women have made in recent years, it's a culture that dictates how

In God's Words

Just then his disciples came. They were astonished that he was speaking with a woman, but no one said, "What do you want" or "Why are you speaking with her?" Then the woman left her water jar and went back to the city. She said to the people: "Come and see a man who told me everything I have ever done! . . . " Many Samaritans from that city believed in him because of this woman's testimony, "He told me everything I have ever done."

— John 4:27-29, 39

But the angel said to the women, "Do not be afraid; I know that you are looking for Jesus who was crucified. He is not here; for he has been raised, as he said. Come see the place where he lay. Then go quickly and tell his disciples. . . ."

— Matthew 28:5-7

What Can a Family Do?

The following are some suggestions offered by Dr. Pipher in her book, *Reviving Ophelia*.

1. Make time to listen to your daughter, especially during the adolescent years.

2. Share your views and listen to your daughter's about the way girls and women are portrayed in movies, advertising, and music videos.

3. Talk with your daughter about what interests her and get her involved in activities that celebrate girls' accomplishments and leadership through sports, school, community, or the church.

4. Encourage your daughter to get involved in activities outside her peer group—volunteer at a shelter, a nursing home, or at the Special Olympics.

5. Don't tease your daughter about boyfriends. Invite her friends—boys and girls—to your home. Get to know her friends.

6. Don't hesitate to communicate your values and what you stand for. Talk with your daughter about how difficult it must be to be a teenager. In times of struggle, let her know how deeply you love her and how much God loves her for who she really is.

girls should look—beautiful, thin, and sophisticated—and how they should act—docile, weak, and nice. As a result, there is an enormous gap between what a girl knows her true self is and what our culture tells her it should be.

Interestingly, girls aren't as susceptible to these pressures in the preadolescent years. They are full of confidence, energy, curiosity, and ambition. But according to Dr. Pipher, something dramatic happens to girls beginning in early adolescence. Although adolescence has traditionally been one of the most challenging times for parents, the cultural changes in the past three decades have created significant pressures and confusion for girls at a vulnerable time in their physical and emotional development. Among some of the observations in Dr. Pipher's book are:

1. A health department survey in Dr. Pipher's Midwestern city showed that forty percent of all girls who lived there considered suicide last year.

2. Eight million women in America have eating disorders. The omnipresent media portrays desirable women as thin, and in the last two decades these women have become slimmer and slimmer. Almost all adolescent girls feel fat, worry about their weight, diet, and feel guilty when they eat. In fact, girls with eating disorders are often the ones who have "bought" the cultural messages about women and attractiveness.

3. Alcohol is the drug of choice of most teens. Many of the messages portrayed in popular culture encourage girls to consume alcohol and nicotine to sedate their pain. Adolescent girls are the only population group whose smoking has increased over the last twenty years.

4. On any given day in America, 480 women and children will be forcibly raped. Thirty-two percent of all rapes occur when the victim is between the ages of eleven and seventeen. Girls are growing up in a world where one in four women will be raped in their lifetime. The incidence of rape is increasing because our culture's destructive messages about sex and violence are increasing. There is a dangerous mixing of sex and violence

in today's music, advertising, television programs, and movies.

Dr. Pipher effectively makes her case for the need to address the dangers facing our daughters, but she also provides proven methods that have helped girls hold onto their true selves during the adolescent years. She discusses the need for parents to listen to their daughters. She speaks of the importance of homes that offers protection, challenges, love, and structure. According to Pipher, "Girls can be saved by a good school, a good teacher, or a meaningful activity. " It's critical to have well adjusted friends and to be reminded through conversation and activities that there is a life beyond junior high. Teenagers need to be proud of something besides their looks. Girls benefit from being recognized through sports, theater, art, school, and music.

I like to think that one of the most important ways that girls can hold onto their true selves in adolescence is through their church and their faith. But we need to ensure that our church is a place that welcomes girls and women, rather than an institution that undervalues, belittles, or attempts to put girls in their place. Our parishes need to be havens where girls believe they can share their gifts and talents rather than hide them. As our culture sends messages causing girls to sell their bodies and souls, our church must send a clear message that real beauty lies in the size of your heart and not your dress size. We need to let girls know that in God's kingdom there are no cliques. When girls feel pain and pressure in their lives, they need to know that they can turn to a loving God who will see them through their suffering.

We need to be a church that teaches girls that Jesus saw women as people who had an equal opportunity to be involved in the work of spreading the Gospel. In a male dominated culture where women were treated as possessions, Jesus treated them as persons. During a time when women were ruled by men, denied their basic rights, and worshipped for their physical beauty, Jesus spoke with them, empowered them, journeyed with them, and

Books You Can Read with Your Daughter

Girls to the Rescue
edited by Bruce Lansky

Amazing Grace
by Mary Hoffman

Boundless Grace
by Mary Hoffman

Madeline
by Ludwig Bemelmans

Anne of Green Gables
by L. M. Montgomery

Pippi Longstocking
by Astrid Lindgren

Girls Who Rocked the World
by Amelie Welden

Girls and Young Women Inventing
by Frances A. Karnes, Ph.D., and Suzanne M. Bean

Girls and Young Women Entrepreneurs
by Frances A. Karnes, Ph.D., and Suzanne M. Bean

Books and Resources for Parents

Reviving Ophelia
by Mary Pipher, Ph.D.

The Body Project
by Joan Jacobs Brumberg

Celebrating Girls: Nurturing and Empowering Our Daughters
by Virginia Beane Rutter

Great Books for Girls
by Kathleen Odean

Mother and Daughter Tales Retold
by Josephine Evetts-Secker

Father and Daughter Tales Retold
by Josephine Evetts-Secker

Conversation Starters

1. How are girls and women portrayed in television, movies, and music videos? What social messages are being sent?

2. Talk about a woman you admire and why.

taught them. Because Jesus reached out to women with respect, they became his faithful friends. They followed him to Calvary and they were the first to announce his resurrection. Jesus saw women as whole persons—their strengths, their weaknesses, their inner beauty, their gifts, their talents, and their spirit. He saw them for their true selves.

Prayer

Loving God, thank you for the gift of girls and women. Help all of us to see the countless ways they enrich our families, our churches, and our society. In our families, help us to focus on what true beauty is and to reexamine cultural definitions and to avoid shallow stereotypes. May we reach out to girls in pain and let them know that you see them and love them for their true selves. Amen.

The First Week of May

"You Gotta Believe"

No one even thought about changing Channel 9 while my grandfather sat in the La-Z-Boy® chair on Sunday afternoons cheering on the Mets in the late spring of 1969. As a ten-year-old girl, I remember wondering how anyone could sit inside on a beautiful day watching a boring game that seemed to go on forever. One Sunday, as I made my opinion known to my grandfather, I remember being instructed to sit down and learn about the game and the players. That particular game was an exciting one, and it was just as exciting for me to watch the colorful cast of players, coaches, managers, owners, and announcers of the '69 Mets. After a few more games, I was hooked.

When the Mets entered the baseball world in 1962, their 40 wins and 120 losses brought them the unfortunate distinction of having the worst record in modern Major League Baseball history. But during the summer of 1969, there was a change in the air. The team that had been the laughingstock of baseball surprised fans and opponents alike, continuing to win against all odds. It was a great time to become a fan and to witness baseball history in the making.

That July, my sister Nancy went off to girl scout camp for two weeks. We exchanged letters and in one she wrote, "What did you think of Neal Armstrong walking on the moon?" It was thrilling for me to see his "giant leap for mankind"—but I wanted to know if Nancy had heard that the Mets were in first place, a feat that to baseball fans seemed more unlikely than a man walking on the moon.

When the Mets clinched the pennant by defeating the Atlanta Braves that fall, they went on to play the Baltimore Orioles in the World Series. Our teacher, Sister Patricia Pompa, a diehard Orioles

In God's Words

Seek the Lord and his strength, seek his presence continually. Remember the wonderful works he has done, his miracles, and the judgments he uttered.

— 1 Chronicles 16:11-12

When he entered the house, the blind men came to him; and Jesus said to them, "Do you believe that I am able to do this?" They said to him, "Yes, Lord." Then he touched their eyes and said, "According to your faith let it be done to you." And their eyes were opened.

— Matthew 9:28-30

What Can a Family Do?

1. Read Old Testament and New Testament stories about people of faith who experienced miracles because they believed:

Moses and the parting of the Red Sea (Exodus 14:21-31)

Jonah and the whale (Jonah 1-2)

Jesus heals a paralyzed man (Luke 5:17-26)

Jesus feeds the five thousand (Luke 9:12-17)

Jesus calms the storm (Matthew 8:23-27)

Jesus cures the ten lepers (Luke 17:11-19)

Jesus turns water into wine (John 2:1-11)

Jesus raises Lazarus from the dead (John 11:1-44)

fan, realized there was no point in teaching social studies those October afternoons. Instead, our class huddled around a transistor radio as we listened to the play by play that captured some amazing baseball moments, including the unforgettable pitching by Tom Seaver.

That season, as the "Miracle Mets" won the World Series title, they captured the hearts of baseball fans everywhere. If there was hope for the New York Mets, there was hope for each one of us. Among my collection of Mets memorabilia, my favorite is a signed picture of pitcher Tug McGraw that includes the team mantra: "You Gotta Believe!"

Thirty years later I am standing on a field of green surveying the newest Mets. They are pitching. They are catching. They are throwing grass in each other's faces. Their greatest concern is what color team shirts they will be wearing. They are six-year-old girls, my daughter's T-ball team. I am, of all things, their coach. (When the sign-up sheet had come around, I had agreed to "help.") But any doubts I had about answering the call to coach were dispelled at the baseball clinic two weeks earlier when I was handed my team roster. It said: Team #1, Lawrenceville Mets. I was hooked.

It was obvious during this first practice that we had to start with the basics. We talked about what it means to be part of a team. We went over safety rules—twice. We talked about being a good sport. Then we began. We stretched. We ran the bases and shouted out the name of each base as we stepped on it. Each girl took a turn hitting the ball off the tee. A few of the girls found out for the first time if they batted righty or lefty.

On opening day, in the top of the first inning, I was asked by three of our players if the game was almost over. In the second inning, I lost half of my infield as the girls left in search of a bathroom. (Casey Stengel never had this problem.) The girls were oblivious to the balls being hit past them because they were deep in conversation or hugging their friends from the opposing team. Girls sat in the out-field and filled their gloves with grass. My shortstop interrupted her turn at bat because she had to make a wish on the "little white fuzzy thing" that was floating past her. Everyone begged to play catcher although the inning was half over by the time they were in full gear. This truly is baseball at its best. It was a field of dreams, though most had nothing to do with baseball. They were daydreams of friendship, fantasy, belonging, and new endeavors.

Somewhere in the middle of the season—just like our namesake of three decades earlier—there was a change in the air. The girls began hitting pitched balls. They were actually fielding the ball and knew what base to throw it to. We were beginning to put it all together and learning to play as a team. The girls were no longer preoccupied with how much time was left in the game or what snack was awaiting them at game's end. They wanted to know if I thought they showed "good hustle" on the field and if I noticed that they were in the "ready position." They stood on the sidelines cheering and chanting for their teammates, "Let's Go Mets!"

On some level, the girls began to discover the beauty of the game of baseball. In a world where we are hurried and rushed at every turn, baseball invites its fans and players to slow down. The game cannot be rushed and for those who are slaves to the clock, this can be very unsettling. It's the slow but steady pace of the game that enables fans to get to know the players—not only their statistics but also their stories of victory and defeat on and off the field.

Baseball can be a wonderful metaphor for the other areas in our lives: family, parish, community, and the workplace. We've all had our times when we're in a slump and we also know the feeling of being in the middle of a hitting streak. We have our days when we come close to pitching a perfect game and other days when the relief pitcher can't be sent in fast enough. We can identify with the player who is

Books You Can Read with Your Children

Women at Play: The Story of Women in Baseball
by Barbara Gregorich

Baseball Ballerina
by Kathryn Cristaldi

The Miracles of Jesus
(Catholic Liguori Book Club)

The Great Shake-Up: Miracles at Philippi
by Marilyn Lashbrook

Nothing to Fear: Jesus Walks on Water
by Marilyn Lashbrook

Hornsby Hit One Over My Head: A Fan's Oral History of Baseball
by David Cataneo

Baseball Saved Us
by Ken Mochizuki

Books and Resources for Parents

A Great and Glorious Game
by A. Bartlett Giamatti

Coincidences: Touched by a Miracle
by Antoinette Bosco

Wait 'Til Next Year
by Doris Kearns Goodwin

Conversation Starters

1. Are miracles just like magic?

2. Do you think miracles only happened at the time of Jesus or do they still happen today?

cheered when he hits a home run and booed the moment he makes an error. Baseball is a game that celebrates the accomplishments and records of the individual player while never losing sight that he is making a contribution to something larger than himself—his team. Baseball is a wonderful reminder for our world today that when you take a remarkably diverse group of people who share a common goal, miracles can still happen. "You Gotta Believe."

Prayer

Heavenly Father, thank you for all the miracles in our lives. Help us to recognize your hand at work when the selfish become generous, the cynical believe, and the desperate become hopeful. It's a true miracle when a person with a hardened heart has found faith or the wounded person finds the courage to forgive the unforgivable. And what a wonder it is when someone who has spent their entire life alienated from you returns to you with faith, hope, and love. Increase our faith to see your love at work in every situation, whether it is the healing of a terminally ill person, or the acceptance of an illness after great anxiety and suffering. Both are your miracles today. Amen.

The Second Week of May

Mother's Day is celebrated on the second Sunday of May.

My Favorite Things

From the back seat of our van came the sweet and melodic voice of my five-year-old daughter, Teresa, singing along to *The Sound of Music*, on the tape deck. We were taking an unexpected trip to see my mother and I was trying hard to simply think of "My Favorite Things," but Teresa was having much more success than I was.

Many of my favorite things originate with my mother, and it was difficult to think of her at that moment because I was worried about her. The day before my father called me with some upsetting news. My mother had fallen on some "black ice" in her driveway, breaking her hip and requiring surgery. Teresa and I were on our way to the hospital where she would be for the next four or five days. It was such an unusual feeling to think of Mom in the hospital. My mother is never sick; she's been in the hospital only to have her six children.

My mother will be the first to say, "It's not that bad; this can be fixed." But for the rest of us who marvel at her boundless energy, her zest for life, her enthusiasm for teaching, and her remarkable health, it's almost impossible to contemplate her keeping still. I'm accustomed to having a mother in motion. And as I listened to Teresa sing, it occurred to me that another song from the musical, the one that Mother Superior sings about her young novice Maria, succinctly captured my concerns about my mother's recovery: "How do you keep a wave upon the sand?"

My mother is a giver. Long before volunteerism was "in," my mother was the spark for her own "thousand points of lights" program in her family, church, and community. She taught English as a second language in a church basement. As a Red Cross volunteer, she taught thousands of children to

In God's Words

God loves a cheerful giver.

— 2 Corinthians 9:7

In all this I have given you an example that by such work we must support the weak, remembering the words of the Lord Jesus, for he himself said, "It is more blessed to give than to receive."

— Acts 20:35

The righteous are generous and keep giving.

— Psalm 37:21

81

What Can a Family Do?

1. As a family, volunteer to make a meal for someone in need. Each family member (depending on age) can help to make part of the meal.

2. At Christmas time, participate in your parish's "Giving Tree" or "Toys for Tots" program.

3. Talk to your children about why our faith teaches us to reach out to others. Teach your children about the joy of *giving* without the expectation of *getting* something in return.

4. Practice simple giving in your family. Help a sibling or child with homework or a chore. Children can help mom or dad prepare a meal. Read to a younger sibling or to an elderly grandparent.

swim and dive at the township lake. Mom's special concern for senior citizens led her to volunteer at her town's "Dial-A-Ride" program and for the Little Sisters of the Poor.

One of the ways my mother has made an extraordinary difference is through her twenty-year involvement with the Christian Service Program (CSP) at DePaul Diocesan High School in Wayne, New Jersey. For nine years my mother worked as a volunteer in this program and for the past eleven years she has served as the program's director. In the CSP program, every high school senior is required to give one-and-a-half hours of Christian service each week.

When I look at my mother I see so clearly the person that Jesus asks each of us to be. Without any fanfare or fuss, but always with a happy heart and a childlike spirit, my mother lives out the gospel every day of her life. She sees a need, and using the talents and gifts she's been blessed with, she reaches out and makes a difference to hearts in need of healing and souls in need of soothing.

When Teresa and I pulled into the hospital parking lot, I wondered if my mother, who has given so much of herself over the years, would be able to receive from others during her recovery. As we entered the hospital, I was also concerned that she may be in pain or even look different. Not to worry. For the next three hours, my mother held court in her hospital room as my father, a group of wonderful friends, teachers, and her principal gathered around her. I was so grateful to my father and my parents' friends who brought so much love and humor, champagne and doughnuts to her bedside. My sister-in-law, Alison, who came to take care of mom for a week, said what was in all our hearts: "It makes me so happy to give this little bit back to your mother after all she's done for us."

After the first night of visiting Mom in the hospital, I headed back to my parents' home with Teresa. I felt anxious as I moved through the house without her there. I looked at her chair expecting to see her working on her students' papers, completing the *Times* crossword puzzle, or knitting a new sweater for one of her grandchildren. Knowing my mother's extraordinary good health and her positive attitude about life, I believe she will enjoy many more years of health and happiness. God will continue to work through such a faithful follower.

Still I couldn't shake the thought that—for the first time ever—I saw a chink in the armor. It's the realization that nobody is on earth forever, not even my mother. This of course leads me to the unpleasant thought that I won't be here forever either. But I feel grateful and blessed that I have a master teacher who has consistently shown me in word and example that our faith in God, love of family, and service to our neighbor is what's truly important during our time on earth.

I spoke with my mother one morning three weeks after her fall. She had already graduated to a cane. The walker was history. She was driving and getting ready to go back to her teaching. The doctor was amazed at her rapid recovery, but the rest of us knew better. Later that morning, Teresa and I headed out to the post office to mail my mother a care package. As we drove along, I silently reached back for Teresa's hand and waited until I felt her fingers squeeze mine. And I held on tightly to one of my favorite things.

Books You Can Read with Your Children

The Giving Tree
by Shel Silverstein

As Big as an Egg: A Story About Giving
by Rochel Sandman

The Book of Giving: Poems of Thanks, Praise and Celebration
by Kay Chorao

Kids' Random Acts of Kindness
by the Conari Press Editors

The Kids' Guide to Service Projects: Over 500 Service Ideas for Young People Who Want to Make a Difference (Ages 10 and up)
by Barbara A. Lewis

Books and Resources for Parents

Communities of Salt and Light
by the National Conference of Catholic Bishops

Growing Good Kids: 28 Activities to Enhance Self-Awareness, Compassion and Leadership
by Deb Delisle and Jim Delisle, Ph.D. (For use in grades 3-8)

Conversation Starters

1. Do you think it's better to give or to receive?

Prayer

The following prayer is one that my mother loves and has inside each of her students' Christian Service Journals:

I slept and dreamed that life was joy.
I woke and saw that life was but service.
I served and understood that service was joy.
　　　—*Rabiindranath Tagore*

The Third Week of May

Playing and Praying

The rainstorm is imminent, yet my two children and three of their friends plead with me and another mother to spend just a few more minutes at their school playground. Their playground is a magnificent wooden structure of connected tunnels and towers, but the children seem to spend most of their time at the edge of the woods digging for treasure, inspecting ant colonies, studying squirrels, or excavating for dinosaur bones.

As a gentle mist begins to settle on the kids, they run over to the swings which all have monster mud puddles underneath them following a week's worth of rain. With their stomachs on the swings and their feet kicking back like mules, they squeal with delight as the mud plops into their hair and faces. Their clothes and bodies look like they've been dipped in chocolate cake batter. A steady rain is now falling and, as five little children are soaring through the mud and muck, they raise their heads high as if to salute the skies for this unexpected pleasure.

Their excitement is contagious and, as they drink up the raindrops, I can't help but think, "What joy! What freedom! . . . . What a lot of laundry!" As I glance over at the mother of six-year-old Matthew, she seems to be enjoying this moment as much as her son, even after I dutifully mention the mess we have ahead of us. With a mischievous grin of her own, she already knows what the rest of us may need to discover—mud is good for a child's soul.

In an age of electronic toys, elaborate playground equipment, and sophisticated video games, it's reassuring to see that children still prefer to spend most of their time playing with mud, water, sticks, rocks, and sand. Like most parents, I have far too many plastic crates of the more expensive toys

In God's Words

Thus says the Lord of hosts: Old men and old women shall again sit in the streets of Jerusalem, each with staff in hand because of their great age. And the streets of the city shall be full of boys and girls playing in its streets.

— Zechariah 8:4-5

Rejoice, young man, while you are young, and let your heart cheer you in the days of your youth.

— Ecclesiastes 11:9

"Truly I tell you, whoever does not receive the kingdom of God as a little child will never enter it."

— Mark 10:15

What Can a Family Do?

1. Take walks in the rain and splash in mud puddles. When you're through, make mud pies.

2. Encourage your children to finger paint, play with clay, write their own stories and songs, build a fort, play "let's pretend," or just be silly.

3. Allow time for free, unstructured play in your child's day. Stop what you're doing from time to time and join in the fun with your child.

that my children *think* they want. But after the novelty wears off (usually after a few hours), they go back to the toys that challenge their creativity and inspire their imaginations—the box of costumes from Grandma's attic, the dominoes from Grandpa, a fort made from blankets, a sandbox, paints, chalk, building blocks, a musical instrument. Not only are these toys and activities good for a child's playful spirit, they are essential for a child's intellectual and emotional development.

Author Ellen Ruppel Shell (*Smithsonian*, July 1994), describes what makes a playground a success from a child's point of view. "The idea that creative play fulfills a vital need in children has been batted around by theorists for more than a century, but has only recently become part of mainstream thinking in the United States. Americans tend to underestimate the importance of play, to consider it as discretionary rather than essential to child development. Roger Hart (an environmental psychologist who edits the quarterly journal *Children's Environments*) says, 'We all know that children need water, sand, and loose parts to build with, as tools of communication and interaction. Yet most playgrounds have little beyond pieces of manufactured exercise equipment selected from catalogs. Kids don't need equipment, they need opportunity."

Creating a stimulating play space for children in today's world carries a real urgency. An estimated 33.5 million Americans live in poverty, many of them children. A child who is poor goes without toys and often their playgrounds—if they exist at all—are terrifying places to be. Yet, these children at risk have the greatest need to escape to a safe haven where they can create their own worlds, dream their dreams, and soothe their souls.

Many of today's children are growing up in a world where their play time is structured and their schedule of activities requires a personal secretary and chauffeur. The "free play" that was an integral part of many of our childhoods has vanished. But in today's frenetic and sometimes frightening world, a child's need to play freely and creatively is more important than ever.

To be close to a child at play is to be close to God. When we look at our world through the eyes of a child, we too can believe that elves live in the holes made by the falling pine needles; we can believe that a dandelion is a beautiful flower, even though adults say it's a weed. To look at the world through a child's eyes is to question all the mysteries of the universe—why does a robin have a red tummy, where does a spider keep its poison, and how do the flowers know it's time to start blooming?

Playing and praying actually have much in common. In prayer we truly believe in a creator of our world, even though we've never seen God. We embrace the beauty and uniqueness of all God's people, even when others may tell us a thousand times that some people and some things are inferior. In prayer we too can question God about the reasons for all the good and bad that comes into our lives and our world.

When we crouch down on our knees like a child busy at play, it's so much easier to give thanks to God for the exquisite details in nature, the remarkable beauty of our world, and the gift of five monster mudholes in the middle of May.

Books You Can Read with Your Children

Mud Pies and Other Recipes
by Marjorie Winslow

The Foolish Frog
by Pete and Charles Seeger

In the Night Kitchen
by Maurice Sendak

Little Cloud
by Eric Carle

All Dr. Seuss' Books
by Dr. Seuss

Clap Your Hands
by Lorinda Bryan Cauley

The Dandelion Seed
by Joseph Anthony

Play With Me
by Marie Hall Ets

The Best Way to Play
by Bill Cosby (Little Bill Books for Beginning Readers)

Conversation Starters

1. What games do you like to play?

2. Where is your favorite place to play? If you designed a playground, what would it look like?

3. Do you think Jesus played when he was little?

Prayer

Gracious God, you created a world of beauty for all your children to enjoy. With wonder and awe, let us always see your world through the eyes of a child. In our busy and structured lives, help us stop for a moment to remember that praying and playing should be an important part of our day. We ask this through Christ our Lord. Amen.

The Fourth Week of May

"Let the Games Begin"

"Mom, do we have a chess game?" my son, Bobby, asked me one day after kindergarten. "I played it during 'choice time' at school today and I really liked it." It had been years since I played chess and I wasn't sure if we owned a chess game. So I headed down to the basement and looked through the mountain of my old board games. Sure enough, there at the bottom of the pile was a worn and flattened box that amazingly still held all thirty-two chessmen and a brown and white chessboard.

As I studied the pieces, memories of outdoor summer chess games came flooding back, but the rules of the game completely escaped me. Not to worry, I thought. I'm sure Bobby doesn't really know how to play chess, and we'll just be shuffling the pieces around the board. But by the time I had finished reading the instruction booklet, Bobby had set up the board correctly and was ready to begin. As his pawns were advancing across the board, I wondered why the kindergarten parents weren't given a chess refresher course. "No, Mom," Bobby admonished me, "The bishop can only move diagonally. Does Daddy know how to play chess?"

The following day I learned that many other kindergartners had joined the rank and file of chess aficionados. Bobby's teacher, Mrs. Lyons, taught many of the children in the class how to play chess. She often began by teaching the children a game that uses just pawns; the winner of this game is the first to push a pawn to the other side. According to "Chess for Children," this "Lincolnshire system" (which began in South Lincolnshire, England) is fast becoming the accepted way to teach people all over the world to play. Mrs. Lyons told me that children feel good about themselves when they play chess

In God's Words

And in the case of an athlete, no one is crowned without competing according to the rules.

— 2 Timothy 2:5

I have fought the good fight, I have finished the race, I have kept the faith. From now on there is reserved for me the crown of righteousness, which the Lord, the righteous judge, will give me on that day.

— 2 Timothy 4:7-8

What Can a Family Do?

1. Make sure that sports and extracurricular activities are fun and enjoyable activities for your children.

2. If you have the time, volunteer to coach or help with your children's activities. If you can't, make sure you feel comfortable with the style of the coach, the teacher, or the instructor.

3. Talk to your children about their activities. Encourage them as they set and achieve goals.

4. When watching sports or other competitive events with your children, point out examples of good sportsmanship.

5. Read books or watch movies that emphasize personal growth and self discovery through sports or other endeavors, such as: *The Lou Gehrig Story, The Big Green, Rookie of the Year, Space Jam, Angels in the Outfield, Angels in the End Zone, Little Man Tate, Searching for Bobby Fisher.*

because they know they are competing in a game that is usually played by bigger kids and adults.

All this is well and good. But as a parent who has seen her two children experience the thrill of victory and the agony of defeat in ways that can get downright ugly, I can't deny that someone is going to win the game and someone is going to lose. As Bobby was learning to play chess, my daughter, Teresa, who was four at the time, was mastering the game of Candyland. She actually stacked the deck of cards in the game so that she was sure to get "Queen Frostine," propelling her to a quick and decisive victory.

Many children try desperately to hold back tears when their opponents triumph. Others collapse in a heap while declaring that they always lose. Children learn early on that winning and losing are a big part of life. How do we teach our children to be good winners and losers?

Mrs. Lyons said that in the classroom they emphasize to the children the importance of working hard and practicing so that one day they will win the game. She tells them: "If you get angry when you lose, you're not only making yourself feel bad, you are also making the person you're playing against feel awful too." Mrs. Lyons' approach stresses that a child's self-esteem is not built on winning a game, but in trying something new and challenging and sticking to it. Winning becomes the icing on the cake.

These are important thoughts to keep in mind as children become involved in sports and other activities where they compete or perform for the first time. Some children may take the field for pee-wee soccer. Others will perform in their first dance or music recital. Still others will enter their first spelling bee, poster contest, science fair, or chess tournament. Competition is very important in the development of children and each young person responds differently to the physical and mental challenges placed before them. Support from parents can often determine whether sports and competition will be fun and rewarding or whether they will be a source of pressure and stress for their kids. We've all seen those cases when a parent's obsession with winning can be devastating and humiliating for a child.

The Wisconsin Committee for the Prevention of Child Abuse developed a set of principles a few years back to assist parents in motivating their children while also developing their positive self image:

1. Teach your son or daughter that success is more than just winning. Help them feel successful when they are improving and mastering skills or giving maximum effort. In this way, parents can help their child accept disappointment and not see losses as personal failures.

2. Remember to praise effort—not just performance—to motivate a child to try hard. The best way to reward is verbally or with a physical response like a smile or thumbs-up sign. Try to avoid money or material rewards.

3. Mistakes are a part of sport and competition and young people will make plenty of them. When your child makes a mistake, give encouragement and, if needed, ideas on how to correct the error in a positive way. Avoid criticizing mistakes. This teaches children to fear failure and to worry that they will not perform well.

4. Show your children that you love and accept them regardless of the game's outcome or how they performed.

St. Paul reminds us that our most important training is to become players in a way of life whose purpose, faith, patience, love, and endurance are rooted in God. The rules and spiritual rewards of this way of life often conflict with society's overemphasis on winning and looking out for number one. We can teach our children that becoming a true champion is doing their personal best to serve God and others.

A few weeks after Bobby learned the game of chess, he began teaching Teresa how to play. As she suffered her first defeat, I waited for the sparks to fly. Instead I heard Bobby say, "Teresa, it doesn't matter that you lost because you're playing a very hard game. Now shake my hand and say, 'Good game, Bobby.'" Teresa kicked the board, though not as hard as usual, and said, "Okay, Bobby, now let's play Candyland."

Books You Can Read with Your Children

Lives of the Athletes: Thrills, Spills (and What the Neighbors Thought)
by Kathleen Krull

Baseball Saved Us
by Ken Mochizuki

Ronald Morgan Goes to Bat
by Patricia Reilly Giff

The Berenstain Bears Go Out for the Team
by Stan and Jan Berenstain

You're a Good Man, Charlie Brown
by Charles M. Schulz

Chess for Children
by Ted Nottingham

The King's Chessboard
by David Birch

Conversation Starters

1. Can you think of a time when you won or succeeded at something that was very important to you? How did you feel? How about a time when you lost or struggled with something that was important?

Prayer

Heavenly Father, we live in a world where a person's worth is often measured by success. Help us to take to heart the words of Mother Teresa, "God has not called me to be successful; he has called me to be faithful." May we learn to be gracious winners and losers in all our endeavors. As we stand on the sidelines or sit in the auditorium cheering on our children, help us to keep the right perspective. Remind us to praise their effort and determination in their activities. Let us emphasize that love, patience, self-control, good sportsmanship, and service are the ingredients needed to be champions of their faith. Amen.

The First Week of June

Back to the Garden

I recall how one spring a few years ago, my children would head downstairs every morning to inspect their dirt-filled paper cups to see if their seeds had begun to sprout.

Each one had carefully selected a variety of seeds: basil, tomatoes, zinnias, and snap dragons for Teresa; beans, zucchini, periwinkles, and peppers for Bobby. As we opened the envelopes, the kids marveled at the different sizes, shapes, and numbers of seeds which they cupped in their hands. They wondered how these brown, black, and tan morsels could possibly grow into the glorious flowers and colorful vegetables that appeared on the seed packets.

On the seventh day, the reliable bean seeds sprouted and the hoops and hollers from the kids echoed throughout the house. Caught up in the excitement, Bobby said, "I love to pick out the seeds. I love to plant seeds and watch them grow. I love to pick the vegetables, but there's no way I'm ever going to eat them!" My vegetable-loathing son didn't realize that my goal in having a garden wasn't a scheme designed to lure him into eating vegetables. I simply wanted him to be able to identify the vegetables by name at the dinner table as he politely refused them and passed them on, rather than pointing in horror and exclaiming, "What's that? It looks disgusting!" Because he has planted oregano and basil for two springs, he now knows that they are spices on his pizza, and he no longer exclaims: "Why is there grass on my pizza?"

Teresa has her own flower garden that she loves to weed and water. She has also kept a close watch on the vegetable garden. It's delightful to see how indignant she becomes after the neighborhood rabbits have nibbled on the garden plants. These days she can relate more closely with Farmer McGregor

In God's Words

And the Lord God planted a garden in Eden, in the east; and there he put the man whom he had formed. Out of the ground the Lord God made to grow every tree that is pleasant to the sight and good for food, the tree of life also in the midst of the garden, and the tree of the knowledge of good and evil.

— Genesis 2:8-9

"Other seeds fell on good soil and brought forth grain, some a hundredfold, some sixty, some thirty."

— Matthew 13:8

He said therefore: "What is the kingdom of God like? And to what should I compare it? It is like a mustard seed that someone took and sowed in the garden; it grew and became a tree, and the birds of the air made nests in its branches."

— Luke 13:18-19

What Can a Family Do?

1. As a family, plant seeds in paper cups, in a window box, or in a garden plot you've cleared out together. Involve your children in the watering and weeding of the garden.

2. Offer to rake or weed the yard of an elderly neighbor and plant flowers in the spring and fall.

3. Take part in a community clean-up day.

4. Talk to your children about why we recycle and do our best to take care of the earth. Read them the story of creation from the book of Genesis.

than with Peter Rabbit as she announces: "Those bad bunnies better stay out of my garden!"

My husband, Joe, and I planted our first vegetable and flower garden the year we were married. We soon discovered what many veteran and amateur gardeners have found: spending time in a garden brings greater peace, patience, and produce into your life. It's also a wonderful way to spend time with your kids and teach them about nature and their role in helping plants to grow.

In a *Los Angeles Times* article, "Linking Soil and Soul," writer Janet Kinosian quotes the experts on the many positive effects of gardening, among them:

1. One hour in the garden will reduce your blood pressure the same as if you had meditated for an hour;

2. Numerous hospitals and correctional agencies report dramatic decreases in violent and antisocial behavior when gardening is part of their program;

3. Gardening is the one art that stimulates all of the senses;

4. Physiologists report heightened muscle relaxation, slower breathing, and increased endorphin production among gardeners;

5. Psychologists say self-esteem, patience, and generosity are boosted when people garden.

We live in a world where our wonder is often directed at the technological rather than the natural. We extol the marvel of the microchip rather than celebrate the miracle of a mustard seed. Countless farms throughout our country have been sold. In some communities farms are so rare that they are visited as tourist attractions. Landscape services with a team of "lawn doctors" will cut, trim, prune, and plant in the wink of an eye, leaving behind miniature lawn flags warning that chemicals have been sprayed. While it's true that we lead busy lives and yard work isn't for everyone, we should find some way to stay connected to our land. More importantly, we need to find ways to teach our children to care for nature and to respect the earth that feeds and cares for all of us.

It's interesting to remember that God was the earth's first gardener as He planted the Garden of Eden. The Old and New Testaments are rich with images, descriptions, and parables about seeds, sowers, gardens, and harvests. Two turning points in human history also took place in gardens. Sin and death came through Adam and Eve in the Garden of Eden; Jesus' passion and resurrection, by which salvation was restored, began in the Garden of Gethsemani and ended in the garden where he appeared to Mary. And of all the symbols Jesus could have used to explain the Word of God, he chose a mustard seed.

That spring, as I watched my children taking such delight in their paper cup gardens, it was a reminder that children often lead us back to what really matters in life. Children understand what it means to be dependent on a gardener's loving care. They know what it feels like to rely on a gardener to give them water to drink and to provide the right amount of sunlight. Like the delicate flowers, they need our time, our patience, and our tender care. They need us to watch and celebrate each phase of their growth. On occasion, they need us to weed out the bad influences that crop up around them. Like garden plants, they can't be hurried. But if we give them lots of love to grow, perhaps they will have a chance to blossom into something beautiful.

Books You Can Read with Your Children

The Carrot Seed
by Ruth Krauss

All the Places to Love
by Patricia MacLachlan

Somewhere
by Jane Baskwill

Sun Song
by Jean Marzollo

The Wonder Thing
by Libby Hathorn

Wonderful Nature, Wonderful You
by Karin Ireland

The Tiny Seed
by Eric Carle

Growing Vegetable Soup
by Lois Ehlert

Flower Garden
by Eve Bunting

Conversation Starters

1. Can you think of something or someone you had to wait for? Was it difficult to wait? Was it worth waiting for?

2. Are there times when we have to wait for God?

Prayer

God, you are the creator of heaven and earth. Each day, we ask that you help our family to grow deeper in your love. When we are restless or anxious, teach us your patience. When we rush and hurry through our busy days, remind us of the need to wait and to watch the growing process. With wonder and awe, we thank you for the people and the world you have created. Amen.

The Second Week of June

June is a month of graduations, weddings, and other life-changing events.

Where's My Blankie?

"Blankie" was pale pink, stained, and literally coming apart at the seams. The hundreds of miniature hearts that once brightly decorated blankie were faded, and its stuffing was hanging on by just a few threads. But to my then two-year-old daughter, Teresa, there was no object more prized than this two-foot by three-foot piece of frayed material. After a fall, following a tantrum, while meeting someone new, or when getting ready for bed, we frequently heard Teresa say, "Where's my blankie?" When she caught sight of blankie, her thumb went straight for her mouth, her index finger hooked around her nose, and suddenly all was right in her world again.

Blankie was a handmade gift for Teresa from her Aunt Nancy and for the first four years of her life, blankie was always at her side. Like pacifiers, teddy bears, "lovies," and other stuffed animals, blankie brought security, permanence, and comfort in the ever-changing world of our little girl.

It can be difficult as well as exciting for children to go through changes in their lives, especially because these changes are occurring so rapidly. "Enjoy this time with your children," many veteran mothers tell me. "It all goes by so fast, and the changes come so quickly."

For parents, change in our own lives can be just as challenging and exciting as it is for our children. But change can also be a time of great anxiety. When we make major changes in our lives, our decisions can get very complicated. The change is no longer limited to, "how will this affect mom and dad," but "how will the change impact the lives of our children." We long for the security and comfort of our safe world, even when another voice is nudging us to move in a new direction and we know that voice is right.

In God's Words

O Lord, I am oppressed; be my security!

— Isaiah 38:14

Comfort, O comfort my people, says your God.

— Isaiah 40:1

Listen to advice and accept instruction, that you may gain wisdom for the future. The human mind may devise many plans, but it is the purpose of the Lord that will be established.

— Proverbs 19:20-21

What Can a Family Do?

1. When you see changes coming, try to be positive and honest as you prepare your children for them.

2. When your child feels insecure about something new, remind him or her of a time in the past when at first he or she was worried or scared, but the experience turned out to be a positive one, e.g., "Remember how worried you were about your first day of kindergarten? And then you met Matthew, and now you two are the best of friends."

3. Point out changes in nature: the seasons turning, caterpillars becoming butterflies, tadpoles becoming toads. Talk about why the changes are necessary. Ask your children what the world and the rest of us would be like if nothing ever changed.

Today's families are faced with many changes and decisions; some are carefully thought through and others come into our lives without warning: one mother leaves her job, another mother returns to the work force; an elderly parent moves in, a child moves out; a baby is born, a loved one dies; one father takes a new job, another father is laid off; one couple marries, another divorces; one family searches for a simpler life while another family seeks more challenges. Change will often bring stress and turmoil into the life of a family even when the change is positive. But change can also bring about growth, self discovery, and a greater sensitivity toward others. We would be miserable creatures if we never changed. Change gives meaning and direction to our lives.

Whenever we are faced with a change, we need to remind ourselves of the importance of prayer and listening to God as we grapple with all the issues involved in our decision. We may stumble, we may even make a change for the worse, but God will always be with us through all the changes in our lives. In the Book of Jeremiah we read, "For surely I know the plans I have for you, says the Lord, plans for your welfare and not for harm, to give you a future with hope. Then when you call upon me and come and pray to me, I will hear you. When you search for me, you will find me" (Jeremiah 29:11-13).

For Teresa's third birthday, I asked Aunt Nancy if she would make Teresa a new blankie. I thought we could gradually introduce the new blankie and use the old one as a back-up in case the new one was left behind or lost. This was a rather sinister idea coming from a mother who had her own blankie for more years than she cares to divulge! Nancy's daughter Nicole sewed by hand a beautiful blanket and matching pillow. When Teresa opened the new blankie she was thrilled and carried "purple blankie" around for the first week. But when the first real crisis struck, only the original would do. She wanted the blankie that had been with her from the beginning, the one that was comfortable, worn, and tattered.

It's hard to know when the time is right to make a change. Sometimes we need to make a change because our lives are coming apart at the seams, or maybe we're feeling a little worn and rough around the edges. We all have our days when it seems like our stuffing is being held together by a thread. Still, the life we have, for all its ups and downs, is all we know. It's our security blanket.

Children and adults need new challenges, new directions, and new discoveries in order to flourish and grow. But often this means closing a chapter in our lives and this can be a very painful process. And as hard as it was to imagine, one day when Teresa was ready, she said say good-bye to blankie as she embraced the next change that came into her life.

Books You Can Read with Your Children

Something From Nothing
by Phoebe Gilman

Dogger
by Shirley Hughes

Charlie Brown
by Charles Schulz

The Very Hungry Caterpillar
by Eric Carle

Charles Caterpillar
by James Haas

Priscilla Tadpole
by Gwen Costello

Geraldine's Blanket
by Holly Keller

Ira Sleeps Over
by Bernard Waber

Jamaica's Find
by Juanita Havill

Hope for the Flowers
by Trina Paulus

Conversation Starters

1. Do you, or did you ever, have a special blanket, a teddy bear, or stuffed animal? If you gave it up, was it hard to do?

2. Does God want us to change or to stay as we are?

Prayer

Heavenly Father, it seems so much easier to be like Linus, clutching our security blanket rather than letting go and embracing the changes that come into our lives. As we look at the beauty of the ever-changing world you created, help us to remember that change is necessary for our growth. Some changes in our lives are painful—death, divorce, loss of a job, and sickness. Please be our security and our comforter during these difficult times. Let us find ways to grow closer to you through all the big and small changes we go through. Amen.

The Third Week of June

Father's Day is celebrated on the third Sunday of June.

God Bless All Fathers

Father's Day, 1989, came in the midst of a difficult time for my husband, Joe, and me. Six months earlier we had gone through a miscarriage together. At the end of Mass that Sunday, our pastor said, "I'd like to invite all fathers and all fathers-to-be to stand for a special blessing." My heart sank, but then Father Sileo thoughtfully added, "And I'd also like to invite any man who would like to be a father some day to stand as well."

Joe stood tall and proud and, as the blessing began, he turned around and reached for my hand. Although we had grieved together over our loss, until that moment I don't think I realized how much Joe wanted to be a father. I let go of his hand and rushed to the back of the church, thankful that my tissues and sunglasses were still in my jacket pocket.

I had prepared myself for the feelings I might have on Mother's Day, at baby showers, and upon the birth of a friend's or a relative's child. I just hadn't prepared myself for the gentle smile on my husband's face as he received this Father's Day blessing. And I began to think that there are many men who want nothing more than to be a good father. Too often, perhaps, we overlook the fact that, in growing numbers, men too are struggling with the loss of a child, the inability to conceive a child, and the demands of balancing careers and children.

The news stories of fatherless children living in poverty and "Deadbeat Dads" who refuse to pay for basic support of their children grab today's headlines and can sometimes give fatherhood a bad rap. These stories should remain on the front page because there is nothing more reprehensible than a parent who denies responsibility or withholds support and love from his or her own child.

In God's Words

"Honor your father and mother"—This is the first commandment with a promise: "so that it may be well with you and you may live long on the earth." And, fathers, do not provoke your children to anger, but bring them up in the discipline and instruction of the Lord.

— Ephesians 6:2-4

Listen, children, to a father's instruction, and be attentive, that you may gain insight; for I give you good precepts: do not forsake my teaching. When I was a son with my father, tender, and my mother's favorite, he taught me, and said to me, "Let your heart hold fast my words, keep my commandments, and live."

— Proverbs 4:1-4

"Those who honor their father will have joy in their own children, and when they pray they will be heard. . . . For a father's blessing strengthens the houses of the children."

— Sirach 3:5, 9

What Can a Family Do?

1. Pray the Our Father together.

2. Invite a fatherless child that you know to a ball game, over for dinner, or out to a movie with your family.

3. Make time for a "Day Out with Dad" once a month.

4. Be encouraging and supportive to those fathers who make a special effort to spend time with their children.

5. Invite Dad to your classroom, scout meeting, or other activity to talk about something you did together.

There are, however, many fathers who aren't making news but who are making sacrifices so that they will be able to spend more time with their children. Many fathers have turned down a job because it would take too much time away from their family. It's not uncommon for a father to take a personal day from work to volunteer as a chaperone on a class trip. More fathers are asking for paternity leave. Increasingly, fathers are taking an active role and enriching the lives of their children.

My husband's best friend, a writer and teacher, stayed home full-time with his daughter until she went to nursery school. I imagine many mothers who watched him were envious of the way he helped to raise a confident and intelligent little girl. One of my son's best friends has a dad who stays home with him and his six-month-old sister during the day and then works as a contractor three evenings a week. Both children are thriving with all the love and attention from their dad.

These are not the typical cases, but many fathers are realizing that volunteering at their child's school once a month, coaching their child's soccer team, or spending weekend afternoons at the park can be a real boost to family life. Children need time with their parents more than any other activity in their day.

We pay a lot of lip service to putting children and families first. We need to support and encourage men and women who are quietly living out this commitment through their actions. There are also many men who don't know what it means to be a good father. Perhaps there was no example in their own home. We have an obligation to reach out to fathers in crisis through programs of education and outreach before children suffer abuse or neglect.

There are also children without fathers whom we can reach out to so they will know love and compassion in their lives. When I first met Joe, we were both students at Boston College. Once a week he volunteered his time to help a fatherless eight-year-old boy through the Big Brothers Association of Boston. During the time we have known Chris, he and his mom have become very special in our lives. When we left Boston, Joe kept in touch with Chris through phone calls and letters. We always enjoy hearing about his latest girlfriends, his itching to get a place of his own, his jobs, and his dreams for the future. I believe with all my heart that because Chris has been surrounded by people who care, one day he will be a wonderful father, just like his Big Brother Joe.

I feel my own children are blessed to have a father like Joe. He's always there for the big events in their little lives. He makes a date to have lunch with our daughter at school and he volunteers to coach our son's Little League and soccer teams. Each day he delights in hearing every detail of the kids' day and can get just as silly as they can. In many ways, Joe is still a big kid himself. There are moments when I'm watching Joe playing with our two children when I wonder if he will ever make the final step into adulthood. I hope for the kids' sake and mine that he never does. It's what I love best about him.

I knew during Mass on that Father's Day that one day Joe would be a wonderful father. No, he's not perfect, but only with our Heavenly Father does fatherhood reach perfection. On the day our son, Bobby, was born Joe wrote, "Robert Francis was born at 6:51 a.m. Wet, rainy night. A long, endless night of painful labor for Eileen—but in the morning, wondrous joy and glory, our eight-pound boy. I already know this is a special child. It's a paternal instinct, but I think he understands so much already—about us, about the world around him. When Bobby was delivered, I was shaking. I was unprepared for the emotion and the reality of the new life set before our eyes. Beautiful, beautiful boy."

Happy Father's Day, Joe. And Happy Father's Day to all fathers, all fathers-to-be, and all those men who hope some day to be a father.

Books You Can Read with Your Children

My Dad Is Awesome
by Nick Butterworth

Arrow to the Sun: A Pueblo Indian Tale
by Gerald McDermott

You and Me, Little Bear
by Martin Waddell

Finish the Story, Dad
by Nicola Smee

My Dad
by Niki Daly

Good Hunting, Blue Sky
by Peggy Parish

Just Me and My Dad
by Mercer Mayer

Father and Son Tales
retold by Josephine Evetts-Secker

Father and Daughter Tales
retold by Josephine Evetts-Secker

Owl Moon
by Jane Yolen

Books and Resources for Parents

Fatherhood
by Bill Cosby

A Fine Young Man
by Michael Gurian

Conversation Starters

1. The best memory I have of a time I spent with my dad, or someone who's like a dad to me is. . . .

2. We call God "Father" because. . . .

Prayer

Heavenly Father, we thank you for all the love you have shown to us, your children. We thank you for your most precious gift of all—the gift of your Son. Please help all Fathers as they teach, guide, and nurture their children. Let us never forget those children without fathers and our responsibility to reach out to them. As today's fathers feel the stress and pressures of balancing work and family, give them the wisdom to see that their most important job is teaching their children to love you and your ways. Amen.

The Fourth Week of June

The Sad Man

"Why is that man so sad?" my niece, Patty, asked her mother as she noticed a small, bearded homeless man while walking to their neighborhood 7-Eleven store. "He is sad because he doesn't have a home to live in or food to eat," her mother Alison answered.

The answer seemed to satisfy three-year-old Patty, and her mother was relieved that at least this time her inquisitive daughter didn't ask, "*Why doesn't he have a home or food?*" Alison said to me, "This man looks like he could be any child's grandfather; what would I have told her?" Now each time they walk to the store Patty asks, "Will the sad man be there, or has he found a home yet?"

A few weeks later, my son, Bobby, who was also three years old, was closely studying a photograph on the front page of our daily newspaper. It was a picture of a child near death, being held by his mother as they waited for food and medicine in a Somalian relief camp. Pointing to the child, Bobby asked, "What happened?"

Another hungry human being, another person in search of a home. How do you explain something to your child that you don't fully understand yourself? That evening, and every evening since, we have said special prayers for all the children who are hungry. We also began packing grocery bags of food for our parish's pantry for the poor. I wondered what was registering in the hearts and souls of these three-year-old cousins who were learning about the homeless and hungry of the world at such an early age.

For more than thirty years, Robert Coles, a professor of psychiatry and medical humanities at Harvard University, has been recording conversations with children of all faiths and cultures

In God's Words

For he delivers the needy when they call, the poor and those who have no helper. He has pity on the weak and the needy, and saves the lives of the needy.

— Psalm 72:12-13

"Is not this the fast that I choose: to loose the bonds of injustice, to undo the thongs of the yoke, to let the oppressed go free, and to break every yoke? Is it not to share your bread with the hungry, and bring the homeless poor into your house?"

— Isaiah 58:6-7

What Can a Family Do?

1. Bake a cake with your kids and share it with a lonely neighbor.

2. Volunteer once a week, once a month, or once a year to help someone in need.

3. Donate food, clothing, or your time to Catholic Charities or other organizations that reach out to people in need.

4. Read books with your children that tell the story of people without a home.

5. Help your children to become aware that there are people in this world who do not have a place to call home and are never sure where their next meal will come from.

6. As a family, sponsor a needy child through an organization like Compassion International (by contributing $24 a month your family can help provide food, shelter, and an education for a child in need).

throughout the world. In his fascinating and passionate book, *The Spiritual Life of Children*, Professor Coles explores the unique questions, thoughts, and ideas that children have about God and spirituality.

Professor Coles shares a conversation he had with Dorothy Day, co-founder of the Catholic Worker Movement, back in the 1950s:

> I think my pilgrimage began when I was a child, when I was seven or eight. . . . I have a memory and to me it's the start of my life, my spiritual journey. I'm sitting with my mother and she's telling me about children like me who don't have enough food—they're dying. I'm eating a doughnut I think. I ask my mother why other children don't have doughnuts and I do. . . . I asked her if God knew someone nearby, or if he could help us with our modest doughnut plan—to give to the hungry some of our abundance! I was a child with spiritual worries or concerns—and don't we all have them, I hope, and they start earlier than we think.

These days the questions from our children about the poor and the oppressed are coming a lot earlier than at seven or eight years old. Our society is one where the homeless live in our neighborhoods, the plight of refugees from countries ravaged by war is broadcast nightly on the news, and racism at its ugliest is captured for all to see on home video cameras. It seems that we no longer have the luxury of teaching our children about social justice issues when we believe they are ready to grasp the concepts. Even as we are vigilant in shielding our very young children from the violence and pain of the world, there is still so much suffering that we can not always control what they will see. We should be ready with answers to some of the most difficult questions our children will ask us.

When children are taught about the poor, the hungry, and the oppressed of the world, their responses are often so compassionate and so genuine. Perhaps it is because they are still so vulnerable themselves that they understand something about those who are the most vulnerable in our society. They know what it is like to be dependent on someone else for food and shelter.

I know many families who take their older children to serve at soup kitchens, or to visit nursing homes so they can begin to learn about our responsibilities for helping others. Many suburban parishes have exchanges with city parishes so people in both settings have the opportunity to be exposed to different cultures and different ways of life. I believe that the real hope for restoring peace and compassion to our world is to teach children at an early age that Jesus loves the poor and the oppressed, and that when we take care of them, we are taking care of Jesus too.

A few weeks after Patty first saw "the sad man," a homeless man was found dead in a creek at the park where Bobby and Patty play pirates and look for buried treasures. They, rather than an early morning jogger, might have discovered yet another "sad man." Or perhaps they would hear about what happened from other children at the park. I wondered what I might say to them later, if they began asking questions about this senseless tragedy.

I hope I would have remembered to say what our faith teaches us: "The sad man is happy now because he is with God. At last he has found a home and he will never be hungry again."

Books You Can Read with Your Children

The Lady in the Box/ La Senora de la Caja de Carton
by Ann McGovern

Home Is Where We Live: Life at a Shelter Through a Young Girl's Eyes
by B.L. Groth

Fly Away Home
by Eve Bunting

Someplace to Go (Grades 3-5)
by Maria Testa

Home: A Collaboration of Thirty Distinguished Authors and Illustrators of Children's Books to Aid the Homeless
edited by Michael J. Rosen

Books and Resources for Parents

Teresa of the Poor
by Renzo Allegri

Dorothy Day: Selected Writings
edited by Robert Ellsberg

Words to Love By . . .
by Mother Teresa

Heart of Joy: The Transforming Power of Self-Giving
by Mother Teresa

Work of Love (Videotape of Mother Teresa's work with the sick and dying in India)
from Ave Maria Press

The Fisher King (Videotape)
from Columbia TriStar Home Video

Conversation Starters

1. Why is your home special to you? Do you know of families who are without a home? Can you think of how you could help a family who is homeless?

2. When Jesus was born, his parents were homeless. How does Jesus tell us we should take care of those without a home?

Prayer

Prayer for Peace and Justice

God, source of all light,
we are surrounded by the darkness of the injustices experienced by your people,
the poor who are hungry and who search for shelter,
the sick who seek relief,
and the downtrodden who seek help in their hopelessness.

Surround us and fill us with your Spirit who is Light.
Lead us in your way to be light to your people.
Help us to be salt for our community as we share your love with those caught in the struggles of life.

We desire to be your presence to the least among us
and to know your presence in them
as we work through you
to bring justice and peace to this world in desperate need.

We ask this through our Lord Jesus Christ, your Son, who lives and reigns with you and the Holy Spirit, one God, for ever and ever.
Amen.

From *Communities of Salt and Light*
Department of Social Development and World Peace
United States Catholic Conference

The First Week of July

Independence Day is celebrated July 4.

Roots and Wings

"I do it myself!" my then two-and-one-half-year-old daughter Teresa exclaimed as she stamped her feet mightily and threw herself on the floor. She hopped up, grabbed the white shoe I was attempting to unbuckle for her, and hurled it across the room. As the shoe ricocheted off the couch and almost hit our dog, I looked at her in disbelief. "Don't look at me," she said softly as she turned her cheek away until it rested on her shoulder. She walked over to the shoe, picked it up, and proceeded to unbuckle it—by herself.

A child's need for independence is expressed as subtly as a little hand gently urging to be released from the grasp of a parent or as emphatically as a two-year-old's tantrum. Almost from the day we bring our children home from the hospital, we begin the process of celebrating their milestones while mourning the loss of a stage we know they will never return to. After a few months of total dependence, an infant rolls over and realizes she can do something on her own. A toddler takes his first steps and speaks his first words which give him new ways of self-expression. A three-year-old leaves her parents in the dust as she pedals away on her bike. And when a five-year-old climbs aboard a big yellow bus on his way to kindergarten, he leaves behind more than his parents standing at the corner bus stop.

As parents, we know intellectually that a significant part of our job description is to provide opportunities and assurances that will foster self-reliant children. But we find ourselves balancing our children's needs for autonomy with our reluctance to let go of our control over their lives. We worry that our children may not be ready for certain changes. And we know we can cause just as much harm

In God's Words

For you were called to freedom, brothers and sisters; only do not use your freedom as an opportunity for self-indulgence, but through love become slaves to one another. For the whole law is summed up in a single commandment, "You shall love your neighbor as yourself."

— Galatians 5:13-14

As servants of God, live as free people, yet do not use your freedom as a pretext for evil. Honor everyone. Love the family of believers.

— 1 Peter 2:16-17

"If a shepherd has a hundred sheep, and one of them has gone astray, does he not leave the ninety-nine on the mountains and go in search of the one that went astray? And if he finds it, truly I tell you, he rejoices over it more than over the ninety-nine that never went astray. So it is not the will of your Father in heaven that one of these little ones should be lost."

— Matthew 18:12-14

What Can a Family Do?

1. Watch the movie *1776* as a family and talk about why our country's Founding Fathers fought so hard for independence. Do we take our freedom for granted today?

2. Read the story of Moses and the Israelites (Exodus 3-15). Discuss how it must have felt to be slaves under the Pharaoh's rule.

3. Read the story of the Prodigal Son in the New Testament (Luke 15). Why is the Father joyful rather than angry that the son has returned home?

4. Are there people in our world today who do not have their freedom? Are there ways we can help them?

5. Together, write a "Family Bill of Rights."

when our hovering impedes our children's necessary development. The difficulty for parents of young children is often trying to determine what will be a step forward in a child's independence and what will be a sure way to spend the afternoon in an emergency room.

During the summer season I find it easy to compare the art of parenting with that of kite flying. It's a bit tricky to release the precise amount of string so the kite can get started. Then it takes some skill to catch just the right wind so the kite can soar and reach its highest height. If you hold on too tightly the kite never flies free. If you hold too loosely, the kite often takes a nose dive.

All children are unique and some are more spirited in asserting their independence than others. Certain stages of child development are more trying as well. My two children are both in elementary school, but I'm told by family and friends that the teenage years present the greatest challenge for parenting—knowing when to release more kite string and when to reel it in.

As a teenager, I had some heated arguments with my mother about curfews, dating, and parties. I wanted to do what "everyone else was allowed to do." With great delight one Sunday morning, I pointed out to my mother a fitting quotation that appeared in our church bulletin, "There are two lasting gifts we can give our children: one is roots; the other is wings." Of course my finger immediately pointed to the "wings" while my mother's underlined "roots." A few years later, my mother made me an embroidery of that verse. It is still displayed proudly on my kitchen wall. These days, as a mother myself, I find I am more easily directed to the "roots" part of the quotation.

During the times when we get discouraged over the power struggles with our kids, it may be helpful to remind ourselves that as God's children we too play down our need for dependence while asserting our independence from him. There are times when we feel we can do just fine on our own. Rather than listening to what God is asking of us, we often stamp our feet and demand to do it our way. As our friends and acquaintances give in to unhealthy behaviors it's easy to shout back at God that "everyone else is doing it."

Like any loving parent, God lays out some simple rules for us. He sets limits and has certain expectations for us. Like typical children, we break the rules, test the limits, and fail to measure up to parental expectations. God gets angry and is disappointed when we don't listen and, yes, there are consequences and punishments for our actions. But the parable of the Prodigal Son lets us know that even when we fail miserably on our own, we only need to recognize our shortcomings and ask forgiveness. When we do, we will return to a parent's loving arms, and we will be welcomed with indescribable joy! "Let us eat and celebrate; for this son of mine was dead and is alive again; he was lost and is found!" (Luke 15:23-24).

I think the story of the Prodigal Son also says that true independence is being secure in the knowledge that although we live our individual lives, we can't do anything in this world all by ourselves. To know real freedom, we need to recognize the roots of faith, family, and community at work in our lives. Only then will we receive the lasting gift of wings which will take us on our own human and spiritual journeys.

Books You Can Read with Your Children

Fly Away Home
by K.D. Plum

Sailaway Home
by Bruce Degen

The Runaway Bunny
by Margaret Wise Brown

Where Does the Brown Bear Go?
by Nicki Weiss

Books and Resources for Parents

The Parent's Little Book of Lists: Do's and Don'ts of Effective Parenting
by Jane Bluestein, Ph.D.

On My Own: Helping Kids Help Themselves
by Tova Navarra, R.N.

Parent/Teen Breakthrough
by Mira Kirshenbaum and Charles Foster, Ph.D.

The Return of the Prodigal Son
by Henri J.M. Nouwen

Conversation Starters

1. Do you think God gives us freedom? Why or why not?

2. Can you think of a time when you felt like you weren't free? What did it feel like?

3. Can you remember a time when it felt great to come home? Why?

Prayer

God of Freedom, you have given us the gift of free will, allowing us to choose right from wrong. Give us also the gift of courage to choose wisely. When we misuse our freedom, we know we can return to you and you will never cut us loose. Please help our family as we try to create a home that provides protection, independence, and love. We thank you for being a loving parent to us, and for giving us the lasting gifts of roots and wings. Amen.

The Second Week of July

Becoming Comfortable With Conflict

It was entirely too quiet in our basement playroom. My daughter, Teresa, who was three at the time, and her best friend, two-and-one-half-year-old, Elliot, were playing with a toy kitchen set when I had checked on them just a few minutes earlier. Elliot's sister, Jilly, and my son, Bobby, who were both five years old, were playing happily upstairs.

I called downstairs, "Teresa, what are you and Elliot doing?" "Nothing," she replied in a voice implying that trouble of epic proportions was brewing below. I ran downstairs and couldn't believe my eyes. They had found a set of Bobby's magic markers and decided to color their arms, legs, and faces with every color in the box. The trail of their artistic frenzy was also left on a few stuffed animals, an Etch-A-Sketch, and a newly painted white wall.

I'm sure parenting experts would tell me that there was a creative way to handle this situation. But it was 9:30 in the morning, I had five hours sleep the night before, and it was already ninety degrees outside. Besides, these little people were old enough to know better. I was angry.

A terribly unpleasant voice forced its way through my clenched teeth, "I want you both to sit on the stairs, right now! You know that we only color on paper. This was a very, very, very bad idea!"

"Well, it wasn't our idea," Teresa answered in a tone much too brazen for a child in a heap of trouble. "Yeah," Elliot piped in. "It was Jilly's and Bobby's idea!"

Jilly and Bobby appeared at the top of the stairs in time to hear the accusation. But even these five-year-olds were able to find humor in watching Teresa and Elliot's attempt to wiggle their way out of this mess. Within a few minutes we were all laughing and everyone was given a sponge to help

In God's Words

Be angry but do not sin; do not let the sun go down on your anger.

— Ephesians 4:26

But now you must get rid of all such things—anger, wrath, malice, slander, and abusive language from your mouth.

— Colossians 3:8

What Can a Family Do?

1. Talk to your children about their anger or your anger. Invite them to think about ways they can change the situation that is causing their anger. Are there specific steps they can take? Can they change their attitude? Let them know they can always do something.

2. Help your children to focus on channeling their anger into a positive release: take a brisk walk, breathe deeply, talk to a caring friend or family member.

3. Talk to your children about St. Francis of Assisi. Read his prayer for peace.

clean up. It's too bad every angry moment isn't resolved this easily. Nothing works better to cure a short fuse than stepping away to cool off for a few moments or finding something funny in a tense situation.

Although anger is a universal emotion, it's a subject many of us are uncomfortable with. Each of us has our own way of handling or mishandling our anger. Some of us bury our anger, others explode over a minor incident. Some people believe it's not right to express anger, others express it to everyone except the person who's the cause of it. Some people walk away the moment a cruel word is spoken and others will stay to an argument's bitter end, needing to have the last word.

Because we live in a society where child abuse and domestic violence affect far too many families, we need to give parents and children healthy ways to channel their anger. As a growing number of teenagers brings guns to schools and lose their lives in arguments over girlfriends, designer clothes, and drugs, we need to teach children effective ways to resolve conflicts peacefully.

Families are under a lot of pressure these days and we can all benefit from learning new skills to cope with anger and stress. If we don't work toward harmony in our homes, how can we expect to end the divisions that tear apart our entire human family?

A few weeks after the magic marker incident, Elliot's mother and I attended an anger management workshop given by Jerry Gross, a professional counselor at the Vienna Family Therapy Center in Virginia. Throughout Mr. Gross' presentation, he discussed some specific and practical strategies for handling anger in families.

1. Know and understand your anger. Are you an aggressor or an avoider?
2. Identify the beliefs you have about anger and try to change those that are unhealthy.
3. Take responsibility for your anger.
4. Take the anger to the one with whom you are angry. Don't kick the dog or yell at the kids.

5. Don't use dirty tactics, e.g., "You're just like your mother (father)."
6. During arguments, stay in the present.
7. Try to avoid the words "always" and "never."
8. Don't fight in the kitchen or in the bedroom.
9. Have regular family meetings and let everyone be heard.
10. Practice "time out" procedures for adults and children.
11. Sign "No Violence" pledges with all family members.
12. Help your family to accept anger as a legitimate emotion. Be more comfortable with conflict.
13. Learn whether your children tend to stuff or ventilate their anger and help them find a middle ground.
14. Affirm your children when they handle their anger appropriately (or try very, very hard to).
15. During the teenage years, try to remember the good seeds you've planted. Trust in all the good you've put into your child.

It's important to remember that anger is often a sign of some unresolved problems in each of us. Do we feel inadequate as a parent? Are we discouraged in our job? Are we overwhelmed and under-appreciated? Are there issues that need to be worked out in relationships with family members or friends?

While we struggle with how to handle anger, it's good to remember that anger isn't all bad. It can motivate us to speak out against an injustice. It can help us to see more clearly those things that we really value in our lives. And if we're angry at ourselves, it might just help us to change a destructive behavior or attitude.

Whenever I read the story of Jesus getting angry in the temple, I am reassured that Jesus not only felt anger, He expressed it as well. It truly is a human emotion. He also made it crystal clear that resolving our anger is so important that he will be in our midst when we are settling our disputes.

Books You Can Read with Your Children

Feelings
by Aliki

Alexander and the Terrible, Horrible, No Good, Very Bad Day
by Judith Viorst

The Grouchy Ladybug
by Eric Carle

My Many Colored Days
by Dr. Seuss

Pierre
by Maurice Sendak

Where the Wild Things Are
by Maurice Sendak

We Can Get Along: A Child's Book of Choices
by Lauren Murphy Payne, MSW and Claudia Rohling

Make Someone Smile and 40 More Ways to Be a Peaceful Person
by Judy Lalli

The Day Adam Got Mad
by Astrid Lindgren

Books and Resources for Parents

A Leader's Guide to We Can Get Along
by Lauren Murphy Payne, M.S.W., and Claudia Rohling

Conversation Starters

1. When I'm angry, it helps when I . . . .

2. We all get angry; even Jesus got angry. Remember a time when you were angry, How did you handle it? What could you have done differently?

A few days after we attended the seminar, Elliot's mother told me that she had been praying for creativity in handling the challenging moments with her children. Something tells me that children, too, like Elliot and Teresa, on some level pray for creativity and assistance in handling the tough moments with their parents. And judging by their response to the magic marker fiasco, I'd say their prayers have already been answered.

Prayer

Dear God, It doesn't feel good when we become angry. We don't like to have those feelings and it's hard to know what to do with them. You let us know that it's okay to be angry but we need to apologize or get things settled as soon as we can. Please help us to express our anger and resolve our differences with fairness and respect. In families that are torn apart by jealousies and past hurts, teach them to replace the anger and discord with forgiveness and peace. We ask this through Christ our Lord. Amen.

The Third Week of July

Questions by the Sea

My family and I were anchored in a small rented motorboat somewhere off the Jersey shore. With plenty of bait, a fish net, two crab lines, and a white plastic bucket, we were ready for an afternoon of crabbing.

As my daughter, Teresa, and I gently lowered one of the crab lines into the bay, we felt the delicate pluck of a crab's claw on our string, signaling it was nibbling on the bait. Slowly we pulled up the line as my son, Bobby, readied his net to scoop up this feisty blue crustacean. "I got the crab, Dad!" he yelled at such a pitch that any sea creature within a mile of our boat must have taken cover.

As my husband, Joe, dropped the crab into the bucket, Teresa turned to me with a look of genuine delight and said, "This is so cool, Mom."

For one week each summer, we return to the sea at Cape May Point, to be refreshed and restored. And it is "so cool" to follow a simpler way of life— at least it seems simpler until I see the beach bags, bicycles, beach chairs, coolers, and boogie boards cascading from our minivan's rear door each time it's opened.

It is wonderful to retreat to a world where sand castles, sea shells, and sailboats fill our days. The complex world we have left behind and all that it values seems insignificant against the backdrop of this majestic ocean.

Our time at the beach in the summer of 1996 was special because two families whom we have known since our children were infants were also renting bungalows nearby. As the shrieks of seagulls and of our children at play became indistinguishable, it was easy to reflect on the many blessings God has showered on our families over the years.

In God's Words

As he walked by the Sea of Galilee, he saw two brothers, Simon, who is called Peter, and Andrew his brother, casting a net into the sea—for they were fishermen. And he said to them, "Follow me, and I will make you fish for people."

— Matthew 4:18-19

"Again, the kingdom of heaven is like a net that was thrown into the sea and caught fish of every kind."

— Matthew 13:47

What Can a Family Do?

1. Talk about the importance of water in our world. Discuss the many ways we use water, including its use as a symbol in the sacraments. Why should we protect this precious resource? Is it easy to imagine a world without water?

2. With your family, take a walk near the ocean, a lake, or a river. Enjoy the beauty and peace that being near water brings.

3. Go fishing!

4. Read the Gospel story of Jesus calling the apostles to be his followers.

But when we biked to the local general store for the morning paper and coffee, we saw the photographs of grieving families on a Long Island beach whose lives would never be the same because they were personally touched by the horror and hate of our world. Summer is a season when people should come to the beach searching for sea shells, not for bodies and black boxes.

We first learned of the explosion of TWA Flight 800 as we were watching an Olympic preview program two nights before we left for our vacation. My children listened to the news reports and, although they didn't understand much of what was being reported, their questions began. "What is a black box? Why are they checking people's luggage?" Bobby asked. "Did it hurt when the people died?" Teresa asked. "I'm going to ask God to send the people back to earth as humans after he sees them in heaven," Bobby told me before bed that night. "I'm going to tell God to give the people a hug," Teresa said.

I told my children that this plane crash is something that's very unusual; things like this almost never happen and that's why everyone is talking about it so much.

On a glorious Saturday morning following our week at the beach, my husband and I began packing up for the return trip home. I turned on the Olympics for Bobby and Teresa who were enjoying many of the game's events that summer. "What's happening?" Bobby asked. "What do they mean a pipe bomb?" A few minutes later our friend's nine-year-old son, Will, rode his bike to our beach house for a final good-bye. I listened to Bobby recount the tragedy to Will. "Someone put a pipe bomb in the luggage at the Olympics and then someone else called 911." Bobby said good-bye to his friend, walked up our front porch steps and said, "Is this unusual?"

As we were preparing to leave the shore I thought about how much Jesus enjoyed the sea. He spent a lot of time traveling by rowboat. He knew how to fish. Sometimes Jesus would sit in a boat and teach the crowd who had gathered on the shore. His parables and miracles often included water, fish, and nets. He understood that these images could teach us about everyday life and eternal life. It was by the seaside that he called his first followers. Along the shore in the afternoon, he fed 5000 people with five barley loaves and two dried fish. In the evening he walked on water and calmed the sea and winds.

Near the lakeside city of Capernaum Jesus spoke these words: "Very truly, I tell you, whoever believes has eternal life. I am the bread of life. . . . This is the bread that comes down from heaven, so that one may eat of it and not die. I am the living bread that came down from heaven. Whoever eats of this bread will live forever; and the bread that I will give for the life of the world is my flesh" (John 6:47-51). That summer we prayed that these words would bring some comfort to the families in anguish.

Although at times it may seem that the world is adrift, if we fasten ourselves to a faith which is anchored in the teachings of the gospel we will extinguish the hatred in our world.

Books You Can Read with Your Children

I Wonder Why the Sea Is Salty and Other Questions About the Ocean
by Anita Ganeri

A Thousands Yards of Sea: A Collection of Sea Stories and Poems
by Laura Cecil

Seashore (One Small Square Series)
by Donald M. Silver

Time of Wonder
by Robert McCloskey

Swimmy
by Leo Lionni

Books and Resources for Parents

Gift From the Sea
by Anne Morrow Lindbergh

The Old Man and the Sea
by Ernest Hemingway

Fishing For Dummies and Fly Fishing For Dummies
by Peter Kaminsky

A River Runs Through It and Other Stories
by Norman Maclean

Fly Fishing in America
by Tom Rosenbauer

Reflections by the Sea (Audiotape)
by William Breault, S.J.

Psalms by the Sea (Audiotape)
by William Breault, S.J.

Talks by the Sea (Audiotape)
by William Breault, S.J.

Meditations by the Sea (Audiotape)
by William Breault, S.J.

Conversation Starters

1. The best vacation I ever had was . . .

2. Water is a symbol of life because . . .

Prayer

Heavenly Father, there are days when the tragedies of life can overwhelm us and threaten our sense of safety. When we feel frightened and helpless, remind us of the words you spoke to your apostles as a windstorm tossed and turned their boat at sea, "Why are you afraid? Have you still no faith?" Help us to be still and at peace, knowing you are there to calm the many storms in our lives. We ask this through Christ our Lord. Amen.

The Fourth Week of July

The Summer of 40

With great dread and trepidation I put on my newly purchased pair of drug store reading glasses and for the first time, faced my family with spectacles on. "Oh Mom, you look so young with those on," said my eight-year-old son, Bobby. "They look excellent," piped in my six-year-old daughter, Teresa. I made a note to remember their kind remarks when I dished out the ice cream later that evening.

All my family members had been heard from except my husband, who is usually more than generous in his compliments. "I'm reserving comment for now," said Joe. Not the response I was looking for. I realized that the conversation would once again return to an ongoing theme of this summer—getting older.

As the countdown began, during the summer I turned forty, I heard more than my share of unsolicited comments about how it's all downhill from here. I'm not crazy about the reading glasses I now require, but I haven't experienced the panic, the depression, and the aches that I'm told I should feel upon entering my fourth decade. Instead, I had some wonderful opportunities that summer to spend time with lifelong friends and family members and to be thankful for the countless ways they have touched my life.

That same summer, my four college roommates and I gathered overnight for the first time in a few years. The way the jokes were flying, we could have easily been sitting around our dorm room in Boston rather than a Long Island restaurant—except for the topics of conversation.

"Do you realize we've all known each other for more than half our lives?" "I've got to get back early tomorrow. It's William's birthday and I can't believe I'm the mother of an eleven-year-old." "One glass

In God's Words

"These forty years the Lord your God has been with you; you have lacked nothing."

— Deuteronomy 2:7

The glory of youths is their strength, but the beauty of the aged is their gray hair.

— Proverbs 20:29

O God, from my youth you have taught me, and I still proclaim your wondrous deeds. So even to old age and gray hairs, O God, do not forsake me, until I proclaim your might to all the generations to come.

— Psalm 71:17-18

What Can a Family Do?

1. Celebrate birthdays in your home by giving a special birthday blessing.

2. Get a copy of the newspaper from the day your child was born. Tell him what was happening in the world and in your family on the day he was born.

3. Take out pictures of the day your child was born and describe how you felt that day.

4. Keep scrapbooks, photo albums, or collages that mark birthdays and other special occasions as your child is growing up.

5. Celebrate birthdays with family and friends. Do something fun together—play at the beach or in the snow. Try something you've always wanted to do. Laugh a lot. Always stay young at heart!

of wine is my limit now." "No; I didn't decide to train for the New York City Marathon because I'm having trouble accepting the fact that I'm turning forty." "I haven't had any health problems whatsoever, although my knees get a little stiff if I sit for too long, and sometimes I get this pain in my back. . . ." "Is it premature to give you a copy of *Menopause and Madness*?" "Can we please have just one conversation tonight that doesn't come back to doctors, aging, death, or the length of time we've lived on this earth!"

The following weekend I was able to visit with two of my closest high school friends, Teri and Erin. Teri, her husband, and two children had just returned from their first year in Indonesia. They had fascinating and sometimes harrowing stories to tell about living through the overthrow of the Indonesian government. Erin had her own fascinating stories to tell of what it was like to be a first-time mother at thirty-nine. As we sat in Teri's family backyard watching our children play, we became acutely aware of the passing of time. It seemed like just yesterday we were dressed in green plaid skirts lamenting how we had the earliest curfews in our freshman class. How deep and strong our friendship has grown through the years.

It was easy to face forty as my husband and my good friend Janet arranged for a surprise birthday weekend filled with family and friends. It was such a warm and loving reminder of what matters most with each passing year: the loving presence of family and friends, good health, a deepening faith, and a growing awareness of self and others. As I looked at a wonderful photo collage that my mother had made for me, I wondered how the baby in the high chair clutching a blanket with her chubby fists could possibly be turning forty.

That summer I took special notice of what our culture tells us we're entitled to as we grow older—a luxury car, a wrinkle-free complexion, a diamond necklace, and a lifestyle free from the worries of the rest of the world. There's nothing wrong in wanting to live long and well here on earth, but to focus on the superficial rather than the spiritual is to miss why God has blessed us with this extraordinary gift of life.

The knowledge that my friends and I have of life at forty has come from times of great joy and great pain. For me, the realization of how precious life is and how easily it could be taken away came two weeks before my twenty-first birthday when I was the victim of a violent crime in Boston. It was much more difficult turning twenty-one that summer than it was turning forty. Every birthday since then I have felt blessed to welcome each new year. Joe has been with me on each of those birthdays and with each passing year he has helped me to see that love and faith are stronger than hate and fear.

Through my friends' life experiences, they too have tried to find meaning in what our time on this earth is ultimately all about. I listened to one of my friends tell me that she would give up everything she has to spend one more day with her mother who died two years ago. Another friend's father died seven years ago and she wondered if she would ever be completely happy again after that. One of my roommates told me about her beloved nineteen-year-old cousin who died in a tragic car accident the previous spring. Through our tears she told me how her cousin had touched the lives of so many young people in her life. A college friend who had been cancer free for five years spoke of the renewed fear she faced after a recent doctor's visit. A friend spoke of the pain of suffering a miscarriage and another was filled with the joy of becoming a first time mom. A dear friend spoke of her gradual acceptance of the thought that she may never marry. Another friend cried at the thought of never having a child.

As I continue to grow older—reading glasses and all—my prayer is "Lord, that I may see." I pray that I will never lose sight of the responsibility I have to reach out to my family, friends, neighbors, and others in need of my help. May I see the need to offer not simply an outstretched hand, but a compassionate heart to those in pain. I pray that I will never become blind to the role each of us has in building up the kingdom of God in our own lives and in the lives of

Books You Can Read with Your Children

Happy Birthday to You!
by Dr. Seuss

A Birthday Basket for Tia
by Pat Mora

Carl's Birthday
by Alexandra Day

A Birthday for Frances
by Russell Hoban

Happy Birthday, Daddy (Gullah Gullah Island)
by Teresa Reed

Alfie and the Birthday Surprise
by Shirley Hughes

Happy Birthday, Moon
by Frank Asch

A Birthday Cake for Little Bear
by Max Velthuijs

A Farmer Boy Birthday (My First Little House Books)
by Laura Ingalls Wilder

Tuck Everlasting
by Natalie Babbitt (Grades 3-8)

Books and Resources for Parents

Dave Barry Turns 40
by Dave Barry

Age Happens: The Best Quotes About Growing Older
Edited by Bruce Lansky

The Art of Growing Older: Writers on Living and Aging
Edited by Wayne Booth

Gold in Your Memories
by Macrina Wiederkehr

Conversation Starters

1. What is the best part about getting older?

2. Think of someone you know who has wisdom. Has it developed and deepened over time? How does this person share the gift of his/her wisdom with others?

others. Please help me to see the big picture rather than becoming short sighted with trivial misunderstandings and disagreements. Let me see clearly that each day I am given is a great and glorious gift. May I never take it for granted. I pray that I will always see that the love of God, family, friends, and my brothers and sisters in Christ is what I need most with each passing year.

Prayer

Recite the prayer in the last paragraph of this week's reflection.

The First Week of August

Home Alone

During the summer that my son, Bobby, was seven, there was a lot of talk about what he wanted to be when he grew up. At the end of one of these conversations, I asked my five-year-old daughter, Teresa, "What do you think you want to be when you grow up?" Exasperated at my failure to acknowledge a statement she's repeated many times during the past year, she said, "Don't you remember? I'm not going to grow up. I like to be little and I don't want to get old!" Bobby responded before I had a chance, "Well Teresa, everybody has to grow up and it's not like you're going to be the only person out of every one on earth who gets to stay a kid."

Bobby can't fathom anyone wanting to stay little. He is jumping into the future—literally. Each day his feet leave the ground as his arms stretch high. He jumps. He shoots. He scores. Like thousands of other children across the country, he wants to be just like Michael Jordan when he grows up, and he believes that by jumping and stretching each day he'll grow to Jordan's height.

All the talk of growing up that summer had me feeling a bit uneasy. For months I had been in major denial over the fact that, come September, Teresa would be going off to kindergarten. For the first time in seven years I would be home alone.

That July, I turned thirty-nine without a trace of age anxiety. But the day we went to Teresa's kindergarten orientation, I couldn't help but wonder and worry about where the time had gone. At every opportunity Teresa insisted that she was going to be a kid forever, but her growing body and mind told a different story. And her budding confidence and independence indicated that my five-year-old was not only growing up, she was more than ready to head down the halls of Ben Franklin Elementary School.

In God's Words

Rejoice, young man, while you are young, and let your heart cheer you in the days of your youth.

— Ecclesiastes 11:9

Bless the Lord, O my soul, and do not forget all his benefits . . . who satisfies you with good as long as you live so that your youth is renewed like the eagle's.

— Psalm 103:2, 5

What Can a Family Do?

1. Celebrate the big and small moments that show your child is growing up. Take pictures or keep a journal of their first day of kindergarten, the first time they ride a two-wheeler, all their birthday parties, the first time they lose a tooth, their first dance, the day they get their driver's license. . . .

2. Look through family photo albums or home videos with your child. Let your child know how proud you are of him or her and the person he or she is becoming.

3. Put aside a special plastic box or container that holds your child's favorite school papers and artwork each year. Look at it together and take note of the progress and growth in the work they are doing as they get older.

4. Encourage your children to work hard to believe in their abilities and to pursue their dreams for the future.

There are milestones in our children's lives that offer us an opportunity to reflect on how swiftly and ably our children are growing up—birthdays, holidays, first communions, confirmations, graduations, and the start of kindergarten. But there are also the more subtle signs in our everyday lives that let us know time is marching on and our children (with the exception of Teresa) will not stay little forever.

The signs that my two children were no longer little began appearing slowly that summer. The "tippy" cups and the colorful plates with a section for each food group were gradually being pushed to the back of our cabinets. We were now all using the same dinner plates. As we packed for our summer vacation that year, we removed the children's bike seats from the back of our bicycles. For the first time, we all rode on our own bikes. A telltale sign for me that life was changing was the request to turn off the kids' sing-along tapes and turn on their Hanson tape—a popular pop music group consisting of three brothers from Oklahoma. And then came the invitation to the kindergarten open house.

For almost seven years I had been home with my children. I was fortunate to have a rewarding professional career before I had them, and I've been blessed to have a profession I can work at part time from my home. I understand the importance of having an identity separate from my children's, but I also recognize that through their world of wonder, discovery, and love, both my husband and I have gained a stronger and more independent sense of who we are. They are a reminder that what matters most is the person we grow up to be, not the profession we choose.

When Teresa stepped into her new world, I'd be stepping into mine. For both of us the possibilities of new beginnings would be endless. Each of us would be doing a lot more reading, writing, and learning. She would be in a new classroom and, thanks to my husband's hard work, I would be in a newly refurbished home office. Still it was difficult to stop the ache that surfaced anytime I wondered how different my day would be without hearing her burst into song each time we hopped into the car. My office might have a new look, but I'd miss my old cheerful assistant who made me paper-clip necklaces and ceremoniously put them around my neck. I would miss our lunch-time walks around the block and the way her hand slipped so easily into mine. Most of all I'd miss all her hugs, kisses, and expressions of love throughout the day.

During our vacation that summer, my husband, Joe, and I enjoyed toddlers exploring the sand and sea. I asked him if he remembered what Teresa was like when she was a baby at the beach. We were both having difficulty remembering. Then I looked over at a baby sleeping peacefully under a beach umbrella. Her floppy sun hat hid most of her face, except for the thumb locked securely in her mouth. I reached for Teresa who was burying my feet in the sand and plopped her on my lap. I pointed to the baby and told her that the baby reminded me of her when she was little. Teresa smiled and I started hugging her, kissing her, and rocking her back and forth. For a few brief moments she was my baby again. "I don't want her to grow up," I thought. "I want her to be little forever."

Books to Read With Your Children

I Like to Be Little
by Charlotte Zolotow

Brave Georgie Goat: Three Little Stories About Growing Up
by Denis Roche

Gabby Growing Up
by Amy Hest

Baseball, Snakes, and Summer Squash: Poems About Growing Up (Ages 9-12)
by Donald Grave

When I Was Little: A Four-Year-Old's Memoir of Her Youth
by Jamie Lee Curtis

Peter Pan
by J. M. Barrie (Videotape from Walt Disney Pictures)

Love You Forever
by Robert Munsch

Books and Resources for Parents

The Best of Free Spirit: Five Years of Award-Winning News and Views on Growing Up
by the Free Spirit Editors

1001 Great Things About Growing Old: Uplifting and True Testimonials (Unwritten Classics)
from Carol Publishing Group

Growing Up
by Russell Baker

Conversation Starters

1. When I grow up, I would like to be. . . .

2. What kind of grown-up do you think God wants us to become?

Prayer

Dear Lord, Where has the time gone? Wasn't it only yesterday when I brought them home from the hospital? I remember being told that the years with my children would go by so quickly. Well, I'm finding out that's true. Help me to be there for my children in the big moments and the small. Let me enjoy these precious years and help me to encourage them as they take on new responsibilities and challenges. As they grow up and go out into the world, may we remember that we are never "home alone." Our children will have a lifelong home in our hearts. Help us to celebrate their many successes and support them when they fail on their road to finding out who they are. Amen.

The Second Week of August

Letters Left Behind

"Well here we are at last. It is all so wonderful! My mind is filled with the most vivid impressions—thousands of them. What before was thousands of miles away is now all around us. I have not time to describe anything now. I must just say that the houses are knocked to pieces quite as effectively as the Sunday papers picture them. Once again I beg you not to worry about me. Just remember that I am enjoying life to the fullest. What may be hardships to others are to me just wonderfully interesting experiences. It is perhaps not right to write in such a light vein of such a terrible war, but I do find it wonderfully interesting and am having a bang up good time and that is all there is to it."

So ended a letter from Lieutenant Madison H. Lewis of New York to his mother and father on April 20, 1918. My mother discovered a copy of this letter while cleaning out our family's attic. My mother's grandmother, Jeanette Hansen, was a first cousin and dear friend of Madison's mother, Hope Lewis. Hope typed copies of the letters she received from her son during World War I and sent them to my great-grandmother and other relatives who were anxious to receive news of her twenty-two-year-old soldier and son, who was serving in France with the American Expeditionary Force.

Along with the treasure of these eye-witness letters from the Front, my mother also uncovered a box of love letters from her grandfather to her grandmother written at the turn of the century. The letters from my great-grandfather Carl were written to my great-grandmother during a challenging period early on in their marriage when they were separated because of his job as an engineer in Montreal.

As I read through these letters with my mother and my husband, Joe, we felt connected with a

In God's Words

In the beginning was the Word, and the Word was with God, and the Word was God.

— John 1:1

"Heaven and earth will pass away, but my words will not pass away."

— Matthew 24:35

You yourselves are our letter, written on our hearts, to be known and read by all; and you show that you are a letter of Christ, prepared by us, written not with ink but with the Spirit of the living God, not on tablets of stone but on tablets of human hearts.

— 2 Corinthians 3:2-3

What Can a Family Do?

1. Research your family history together.

2. Interview a grandparent or other relative on video or audiotape.

3. Encourage your children to keep a journal, especially on family trips or after family gatherings and celebrations.

4. Remind your children of the importance of sending thank-you notes for gifts.

5. Invite your kids to design their own stationery—on the computer or with paints, markers, or crayons.

6. Write a letter to God.

7. Play Scrabble or Boggle with friends and family.

piece of our past. How privileged we were to hold in our hands the very letters that were once in the rugged hands of great-grandfather Carl as he wrote such tender words to his "dearest little sweetheart" in 1899.

As we read my great-grandfather's words on the white parchment paper, a partial story of his life began to take shape—his bout with malaria, his anxiety when the train didn't bring a letter from his "sweet and pretty wife," and his "dearest wish and happiest dream to wake my sweetheart with a kiss each morning and to have you always content by my side," We were touched beyond words. There is something absolutely revealing about a person writing during a time of uncertainty. A latter day reader not only gets a look into a time in history, but also a look into the writer's soul.

I've thought about this recently as more of my family members, friends, and editors communicate by e-mail. It's so quick and easy. As one friend said, "It's great, you hardly have to think what you're writing."

I understand how practical and efficient e-mail is, both inside and outside of the workplace. But as e-mail grows in popularity, it's important to celebrate the power and beauty of the hand-written word as well.

I'm not opposed to technology, and most days I'm not nostalgic for legal pads and pens. I'm equipped with a computer, a printer, and a fax machine in my home office and my children are already more at home with computers than I ever will be. But ultimately, what is most important is not how we communicate but *what* we communicate.

The art of letter writing has played a profound role in our faith. More than half of the books of the New Testament are letters. St. Paul, one of the greatest letter writers who ever lived, used the written word to teach and encourage the people of the churches he ministered to and to all who continue to read his letters centuries later. I wonder if St. Paul's epistles would be as compelling if they had been composed on a laptop computer rather than on papyrus. I have no doubt that St. Paul would have taken full advantage of technologies that could instantly reach large audiences. But would his eloquence be lost on the crowded e-mail thoroughfares?

I wonder too if Lieutenant Madison Lewis' letters from France or great-grandfather Carl's letters of love would have been as poignant if their writers could have communicated so directly and instantly. Through occasional visits, and a pen that wouldn't quit, great-grandfather Carl worked out the difficulties of distance with his young bride by taking a job as an inventor and engineer at Ingersoll Rand in Easton, Pennsylvania. Ultimately he was awarded more than 300 patents, including one for the underwater rock drill which was instrumental in the building of the Panama Canal. Most important to me, Great-grandfather Carl and Great-grandma Jeanette had a daughter who would one day be my Grandma Jean.

And what of Lieutenant Madison Lewis? Four months after arriving in France, the lieutenant was promoted to captain and received the Distinguished Service Cross. The citation reads:

"Captain Madison H. Lewis, 302nd Engineers for extraordinary heroism in action near Ville-Savoy, France, on August 18, 1918. Under enemy fire, high explosives, and gas, Captain Lewis plunged into the Vesle River to rescue some soldiers who had fallen into the water with full pack while crossing a footbridge and were in danger of drowning. In order to do this he removed his gas mask and as a result was severely gassed."

The wide-eyed soldier who began a thrilling journey across the Atlantic to fight in World War I started an inward journey just months later after experiencing the devastation and human suffering caused by war. How do I know? It's all in the letters left behind.

Books You Can Read with Your Children

First World War
edited by John D. Clare

Love Letters Before Birth and Beyond: A Mother's Journal to Read and Keep
by Mary Knight

The Young Person's Guide to Becoming a Writer
by Janet E. Grant

Write From the Edge: A Creative Borders Book
by Ken Vinton, M.A.

Put Your Heart on Paper
by Henriette Anne Klauser

Webster's New World Word Madness Game

It's Your Story—Pass It On
by Mary Louise Colgin and Thea Simons van der Ven

Through My Eyes: A Journal for Teens
by Linda Kranz

Letters to Julia
by Barbara Ware Holmes

Writing Down the Days: 365 Creative Journaling Ideas for Young People
by Lorraine M. Dahlstrom

Conversation Starters

1. If, like St. Paul, you were put into prison for your faith and could write only one letter about that, what would you write?

2. Think of one word that describes each member of your family and one word that describes God to you.

Prayer

Dear God, help us to choose our words wisely. May our words be kind, caring, and encouraging within our family, our churches, and communities. Help us to remember that name calling and careless words can hurt. As we listen to the words of St. Paul, St. Peter, and other great letter writers, help us to remember the sacrifice they made so that your words would be passed on to future generations. As a family, help us to read, reflect, and act upon your word, and bring this good news to those whom we meet. Amen.

The Third Week of August

"I Have Something Very Important to Say!"

A few years ago, at a typically loud and festive family gathering, my six-year-old nephew, Ray, stood and announced, "I have something very important to say!" By the time all the adults had settled down and were ready to listen, Ray was so upset that he forgot what he was going to say and left the room in tears.

I wonder what gem we missed. Just a few weeks later our family was gathered together once more for my brother's wedding and Ray noticed some people quietly praying before Mass began. My husband asked Ray if he knew what the people were doing. "Sure," Ray replied, "they are talking to God in their heads."

There is so much to learn when we practice the art of listening to our children. When we do, we are letting them know that no matter how little they are, what they say and think truly matters. We are showing them that they have dignity and self-worth, that they are children of God.

Parents who listen carefully to their child's thoughts, hopes, and fears are helping to build their child's confidence and self-esteem. They are also privileged to catch a glimpse of their child's inner world, a place without cynicism, hatred, jealousy, or prejudice.

I believe this is why Jesus said, "I assure you that whoever does not accept the reign of God like a little child shall not take part in it." This is an extraordinary statement. It seems to me that if we are really listening to what Jesus is saying, we should be learning everything we can about being like the little children and spending a lot more time listening to them.

This story of Jesus embracing and blessing the little children is one of the most revealing moments

In God's Words

"Whoever listens to you listens to me, and whoever rejects you rejects me, and whoever rejects me rejects the one who sent me."

— Luke 10:16

Let everyone be quick to listen, slow to speak, slow to anger.

— James 1:19

"This is my Son, the Beloved; listen to him!"

— Mark 9:7

What Can a Family Do?

1. Make time each day to ask your child about their day and listen to him or her. When your child is talking, try to stop what you are doing and look at him or her. If you have little children, get down to their level and look at them as they're speaking to you.

2. As a family, set aside scheduled time each week or whenever possible when all family members can be listened to, e.g., a family meeting or going out for pizza.

3. Take a parenting course or read a parenting book. Learn effective ways to talk with and listen to your child so the time you have together has more meaningful conversations and fewer arguments.

4. Set an example for your children by listening to what God is asking you through prayer or by attending church services.

5. Take a walk or a hike with your child. Ask them what sounds they hear.

in the Gospel. St. Mark writes: "People were bringing little children to him in order that he might touch them; and the disciples spoke sternly to them. But when Jesus saw this, he was indignant and said to them, 'Let the little children come to me; do not stop them; for it is to such as these that the kingdom of God belongs'" (10:13-14).

Jesus understood the hearts of children. He delighted in their laughter and their words. How his heart must be breaking as war, poverty, crime, and neglect extinguish the wonder, hope, and trust of little children. Many of today's news stories from around the world and in our own American cities, remind us that not only are our children not listened to, but sometimes their basic needs for food, shelter, and security are not even met.

When life is moving at a breakneck speed, it can be a challenge just to listen within our families. After all, listening takes time, patience, and energy, and all are at a premium in our busy lives. A child's question or thought is easily lost somewhere between rushing to get a meal on the table, buckling a child in a car seat, or hurrying off to get some errand done. There are days when I fear that the words my children will remember most from their childhood will be, "Come on, hurry up, we gotta go."

It is in the simple act of listening that we let our children know that they are loved, treasured, and valued. As our children grow older, it's important to recognize that if we consistently don't find the time to listen to them, there's a good chance they will turn elsewhere and find someone who will. Some children may turn to friends or acquaintances at school. For others, the pain or isolation of feeling that they are not loved can lead to alcohol abuse, early sexual activity, or other self destructive behaviors. Ultimately, we all have something important to say, and we need to have our loved ones listen to us.

As we strive to become better listeners, it's important to remember that no one has perfected the art of listening, not even loving parents. We will make mistakes and come up short in the listening department. But what's most important is that children see that their parents make an effort to listen to them in the midst of all the things that demand a parent's time.

There are times when it's exasperating to listen to children with their endless questions, demands, and ramblings. There is at least one moment in every day when we wish our children would be the ones doing more of the listening. But they are testing us and learning from us. We have much to learn from them too, with their simple yet inspiring way of seeing the world.

Through the Gospel of Mark we learn that it's crucial to understand and imitate a child's way of seeing the world. Jesus has given us a road map to the kingdom of God, and if we are to find our way, we must accept the reign of God like a little child. I know that even with the best road map, I frequently get lost. But perhaps a first step in the right direction is to listen to and learn from my children. Because all children, like little Ray, have something very important to say.

What Can a Family Do?
(continued)

6. One of the best times of day to listen to your children is at night, right before bedtime. Let it be a regular time when they can tell you about their day, talk about their successes or problems or share what will be happening in the week ahead. Before you kiss them good night, say a prayer or give them a blessing that lets them know you've just listened to what they've told you.

7. When you listen to your children's concerns, they don't need you to solve their problems. Sometimes just talking it out with a parent helps them sort things through. Most importantly, it lets them know you care.

Books You Can Read with Your Children

Listen to Me
by Barbara J. Neasi

The Other Way to Listen
by Byrd Baylor

Listen Buddy
by Helen Lester

Listen to the Rain
by Bill Martin and John Archambault

Listen to the Desert/Oye Al Desierto
by Pat Mora

What Happens When Children Pray: Learning to Talk and Listen to God
by Evelyn Christenson

Books and Resources for Parents

How to Talk So Kids Will Listen & Listen So Kids Will Talk
by Adele Faber and Elaine Mazlish

Conversation Starters

1. How do you feel when someone takes the time to listen to you? How do you feel when you have something very important to say and a family member or friend tells you, "Not now, I'm busy"?

2. In our busy days, is it possible to find time to listen to God? What do you think this means? Why is this important? How can you be a better listener?

Prayer

Dear God, you have let us know that whatever joys, hopes, or fears we hold in our hearts, you are never too busy to listen to us. Help us, in our hurried lives, to find the time to listen to your word and to what you are asking of us. May we also find the time to listen within our families and to cherish and value one another by our listening. Help us to be better listeners, to you and to those we love. We ask this through Christ our Lord. Amen.

The Fourth Week of August

A Case of the "Gimmies"

The three-line ad in the newspaper announcing the garage sale failed to capture the behind-the-scenes work and stress that went into preparing for this event.

I had never taken part in a garage sale, but it seemed like a good opportunity to clean house and to motivate my kids to go through their toys and clothes to see what we could give away. I often brought my boxes of clothes, housewares, and toys to a local charity, not because I was a do-gooder, but because I was too tired or lazy to haul out all my junk onto card tables and have strangers come by and barter over my old belongings.

As I began rummaging through our bedrooms and basement, I quickly became agitated over the amount of stuff we had acquired, even after our countless promises to simplify our lives. As I began taking stock of our stuff, I found myself uttering phrases like: "We have too much stuff! Do you kids know there are children in the world who don't have any toys?" In the midst of this frenzy, I called another friend who was also preparing for the garage sale. "Hello!" she snapped uncharacteristically into the phone. "Oh I'm sorry," she said. "I've just come from the basement and I can't believe how much stuff we have."

When my kids were preschoolers, they both went through a stage of demanding a toy or a treat anytime we went to the store. Then I came across the book, *The Berenstain Bears Get the Gimmies.* The two bear cubs had a similar problem that my kids were experiencing—"give me this and give me that." After one outing Papa Bear told the cubs it was the worst case of the "galloping greedy gimmies" he had ever seen. The phrase "gimmies" really stuck in our home and no one ever wants to

In God's Words

Keep your lives free from the love of money, and be content with what you have; for he has said, "I will never leave you or forsake you."

— Hebrews 13:5

"Therefore I tell you, do not worry about your life, what you will eat or what you will drink, or about your body, what you will wear. Is not life more than food, and the body more than clothing? . . . For it is the Gentiles who strive for all these things; and indeed your heavenly Father knows that you need all these things. But strive first for the kingdom of God and his righteousness, and all these things will be given to you as well."

— Matthew 6:25, 32-33

And he said to them, "Take care! Be on your guard against all kinds of greed; for one's life does not consist in the abundance of possessions."

— Luke 12:15

What Can a Family Do?

1. Pray daily for the needs of the poor with your children.

2. As a family, volunteer to reach out to those in need—make a dinner or bag lunches once a month for a community shelter or soup kitchen.

3. Organize a neighborhood or parish drive for diapers, canned goods, winter coats, books, or "back-to-school" items for those in need.

4. Invite your children to donate their money to help sponsor a week of summer camp for a homeless child.

5. Discuss with your children the difference between needs and wants. What are their wants; what are their needs?

be accused of having a case of them. As parents we wonder why our children expect to be given so much while we continue to consume and to be consumed by material possessions.

We are a society with a chronic case of the "gimmies." We have grocery stores with eighteen brands of one product on the shelf. We have a cable TV channel just for shopping. We have catalogs that arrive in our mailboxes almost daily urging us to buy more stuff. No matter where we turn, someone is trying to sell us something we really don't need.

As I sat among my boxes of stuff getting ready for the garage sale, I was struck by the contrasting images on TV of Mother Teresa who had died the day before. Dressed in her trademark white sari with a blue stripe, she was reaching out to the poorest of poor. The only stuff Mother Teresa ever needed on her life's journey were a burning love for Jesus and a joyful and generous heart to serve people in need.

Mother Teresa often spoke of the great material wealth she saw when visiting the United States and how a preoccupation with possessions and riches can easily lead to spiritual poverty. After one visit she remarked, "The spiritual poverty that one finds in Europe and America is a difficult burden to carry. One day there springs the desire for money and for all that money can provide—the superfluous, luxury in eating, luxury in dressing, trifles. Needs increase because one thing calls for another. The result is uncontrollable dissatisfaction."

Mother Teresa also reminded us that if we're so busy filling our lives with the best clothing, toys, food, and furniture, God cannot find his way into our hearts. She often said, "Let us remain as empty as possible so that God can fill us up. For not even God can put anything in a heart that is already full. The more we become empty of ourselves, the more we will be able to be filled with God."

I loaded the boxes for the garage sale into our van on the day of Mother Teresa's funeral. I remember how closely I listened to the words that came from the small woman with the giant heart:

Those who have had many possessions, who have had many goods and riches, are obsessed by them. They think that the only thing that counts is possessing wealth. That is why it is so difficult for them to leave all things as they are dying. It is much easier for the poor, who are so free, for this freedom allows them to depart this world with joy. For my part I must say that the poor are very lovable people, who give us more, much more than we give them.

Books You Can Read with Your Children

The Clown of God
by Tomie dePaola

Peppe the Lamplighter
by Elisa Bartone

Uncle Willie and the Soup Kitchen
by DyAnne DiSalvo-Ryan

Silver Packages
by Cynthia Rylant

The Apple Cake
by Nienke van Hichtum

VeggieTales: Madame Blueberry
(Videotape)
from Big Idea Productions

Books and Resources for Parents

A Woman's Guide to a Simpler Life
by Andrea Van Steenhouse, Ph.D.

The Simple Living Guide
by Janet Luhrs

Material World: A Global Family Portrait
by Peter Menzel

Plain and Simple
by Sue Bender

Words to Love By . . .
by Mother Teresa

Conversation Starters

1. If you could choose your three most valuable treasures from your home, what would they be? Why?

2. What treasures has God blessed you with?

Prayer

Heavenly Father, you have blessed our lives with an abundance of treasures. Most importantly, you have given us the gifts of faith, hope, and love. We live in a world that values money, wealth, and power and it's so easy to get caught in this trap and to fill up our lives with too much stuff. It's so hard to simplify our lives. May our family find ways to fill up our lives with your word and to reach out to those in need. Help us to remember that you will provide us with all we need on earth and in heaven. Amen.

The First Week of September

The Blue Bus

Ever since my son, Bobby, was two years old, singing along to "The Wheels on the Bus," he has anxiously awaited the day when he would ride the school bus. So it was with great excitement that he ran out the door on his first day of kindergarten a few years ago and took his place with all the other youngsters at the corner bus stop.

Although all of the school buses were yellow, each one had a cut-out picture of a bus in a different color which is placed in the front window so the kids could easily identify their particular bus. Bobby was on the blue bus. As requested by his school, he also had his name, address, and bus color pinned to his shirt.

Bobby jumped on the bus with such enthusiasm and confidence that he was gone before we had time to capture his bright smile with the two cameras we brought to make sure we wouldn't miss this important milestone.

"Did he get a seat? Is he okay?" I asked my husband. As the bus pulled away, I caught a blurred image of his face sitting next to a boy with a baseball cap. It was all happening too quickly for me to understand the enormity of this moment. He seemed so happy about every aspect of going to school that I held back my tears.

The return trip was another story altogether. As he stood at the top step of the bus, he caught sight of me and began to cry, "I looked out the bus window and I didn't see you there and I thought you forgot about me and I didn't know where the driver was going to bring me. Why weren't you on the other side of the road?" I hugged him tightly and I began crying as all the emotion of the day caught up with me as well.

"Oh Bobby, I'm sorry," I told him. "We were asked to wait on the other side of the road because

In God's Words

Before he went out to start his journey, he kissed his father and mother. Tobit then said to him, "Have a safe journey." But his mother began to weep, and said to Tobit, "Why is it that you have sent my child away? Is he not the staff of our hand as he goes in and out before us?" Tobit said to her, "Do not worry; our child will leave in good health and return to us in good health. Your eyes will see him on the day when he returns to you in good health. Say no more! Do not fear for them, my sister. For a good angel will accompany him; his journey will be successful, and he will come back in good health." So she stopped weeping.

— Tobit 5:17-6:1

What Can a Family Do?

1. Say a special blessing for your child before she/he leaves for the first day of school.

2. Plan a special breakfast, dinner, or dessert to celebrate the day.

3. Send a note inside your child's lunch box saying you're thinking of him or her.

4. Talk to your child about the day at school. Invite a new friend over to play.

the construction people were doing road work. I was confused about where to go just like you."

"Well, you were only confused about one thing," he answered. "But I was confused about everything today!" He cried even harder than before as he explained, "At school, I couldn't find my blue bus. The patrol boy left me and started talking to someone else. I didn't know what bus to get on and I didn't see anyone that I knew. I couldn't stop crying because I thought I would never be able to find my way home. And there were so many kids. And these people kept yelling out, ' White bus over here. Red bus over here. Green bus come over this way.' And then they yelled, 'ESS Elementary, Takoma Park School,' and then I think they yelled out all the countries of the world."

"But you found the blue bus," I said trying to reassure him and me. "Well that's because I found Will. He's going to be a patrol boy because he's eight. And their job is to help the younger kids. And I said 'Will, I can't find my bus and I'm scared.' So Will brought me over to my bus."

As we sat by the side of the road and talked about his first day of school, I was happy and relieved to discover that except for his search for the elusive blue bus, he had a wonderful time during his first day of kindergarten. He then began a lively discussion about how much he liked his teacher and the three new friends he made.

After I put Bobby to bed that night, I realized that he had begun a whole new journey involving much more than a bus ride. It marked a new adventure for my husband and me too. That first day of school was the first of many days when Bobby would ride off confidently and carefree as he begins a new stage in his young life. It was also a reminder that there are sure to be other days when he'll struggle to find his way in a world that at times seems confusing and overwhelming. As adults, we too have our days when we feel excited and hopeful about new opportunities and challenges. We also have our share of days when we're frightened and vulnerable. We still know how good it feels to find a friend extending a smile and a helping hand when we've lost our way.

That evening, for the first time in months, Bobby woke up with a terrible dream. He couldn't find his bus. I read him the letter I had written to his teacher to let him know we would make sure he got on the bus with no trouble. A tear that felt like the size of a school bus slid down my cheek and splashed on to his arm. "Oh Mom," he said. I held him until he fell asleep.

The following day I couldn't stop thinking about Bobby. I took my friend Chris' advice and prayed for him whenever my own fear and worry settled in. It was my only way of being connected with him throughout the day and it brought me peace.

That afternoon, Bobby's sister, Teresa, and I met him at the bus stop. He smiled from the top step and I knew that all went well. As we walked home he said, "The hardest thing in school is staying inside the tape that the teacher puts down. If you go outside the tape she could accidentally step on you when she's reading a story. The worst part about school is that sometimes you have to lie down after lunch even if you're not tired. But the best thing about going to school is walking up the black steps onto the blue bus and sitting next to my new friend Patrick."

Books You Can Read with Your Children

Franklin Goes to School
by Paulette Bourgeois

Miss Bindergarten Gets Ready for Kindergarten
by Joseph Slate

Froggy Goes to School
by Jonathan London

Lily's Purple Plastic Purse
by Kevin Henkes

Boomer Goes to School
by Constance W. McGeorge

Spot Goes to School
by Eric Hill

Oh, the Places You'll Go
by Dr. Seuss

Grover Goes to School
by Dan Elliott

Conversation Starters

1. Can you remember when you visited a place for the first time? What helped you to feel comfortable? What's the farthest journey you have ever taken?

2. How do you think God gives us courage as we begin new journeys and adventures in our lives?

Prayer

Dear Lord, help us to remember that you are with us as we begin all our journeys in life, no matter how big or small. If we stumble, or lose our way, give us the courage to hang in there. Help us to see that each time we begin a new journey we are presented with new challenges and opportunities to grow. Give us the confidence to hop on the many "blue busses" that will come into our lives. On all our journeys may we never lose sight that you are journeying with us. We ask this through Christ our Lord. Amen.

The Second Week of September

September is Hispanic Heritage Month.

"Hola Means Hello"

It usually happens while I'm sitting at my kitchen table; I get a funny feeling that someone is watching me. I glance out my casement window, into the picture window across the street and discover the source of my suspicion.

A white curtain in the picture window is drawn back and lifted like a woman gathering her flowing skirt. It reveals the faces of four, five, sometimes six children whose dark eyes brighten as we make contact across the great divide of our busy street. The children's voices holler cheerfully out the open window, "Hola! Where are your children? What are you going to do today?"

No matter how many times this scene is repeated, it's a sight I always welcome. The children, seven in all, and their parents, left their homeland of El Salvador and settled in our neighborhood.

For the first few months after the Alvarez family moved in, we exchanged pleasant greetings each time we passed. We welcomed the family with food, housewarming gifts, and a present for the new baby. As the months went by, I thought I was being a model neighbor until my son, Bobby, asked one day, "Mom, how come the kids from across the street have never come over to our house to play?"

"How come?" I wondered myself. Was language our only barrier? The next day I took my two children across the street and knocked at the Alvarez door. Ilsia, Dina, Juan, Axa, Abner, and Samuel met us at the door and invited us into the living room so we could talk with their mother, Maria.

I began speaking to Maria in Spanish, and my Spanish was rusty to say the least. All the children were convulsed in laughter at the sound of Bobby

In God's Words

"Whoever welcomes you welcomes me, and whoever welcomes me welcomes the one who sent me."

— Matthew 10:40

Welcome one another, therefore, just as Christ has welcomed you, for the glory of God.

— Romans 15:7

What Can a Family Do?

1. Trace your family's heritage. What countries did your family come from? Where did they live when they first arrived in America? How were they treated?

2. Watch the movie *An American Tail* (Universal Pictures) and talk about what it must feel like to journey to a new land.

3. Next month we celebrate United Nations Day. Learn about a country where your ancestors came from. Make a meal or dessert from that country.

4. As a family, go out for an occasional meal to an ethnic restaurant.

5. As a family, learn more about Catholic Relief Services and other organizations that reach out to those in need around the world.

and Teresa's mommy speaking Spanish. "You sound so funny!" they all laughed. A few minutes later all the kids disappeared upstairs to play on a colorful hammock that the family had brought with them from El Salvador. As Maria and I listened to the children squealing with delight upstairs, we both smiled. It seems that children play the same in every language. And, downstairs, as we talked about the children's bee stings, past pregnancies, and the upcoming school year, it was clear that mothers everywhere speak the same language too. Since that afternoon, our children often play together, and they attend the same school. My family has received the extraordinary gift of the culture, spirit, and friendship of this Hispanic family.

Our lives have also been enriched these past few weeks with the rich diversity of Hispanic, African-American, Asian, and American children who attend my son's elementary school. Through the school's special programs, curriculum, and celebrations, there is a respect and openness to children of all cultures, races, and religions.

When my son was in kindergarten, his class celebrated Hispanic Heritage Month with a fiesta in the classroom. It was a real delight listening to Bobby's description of the food they tasted, the music they danced to, and the people they learned about. Bobby said, "I know how to count to ten in Spanish. I ate this kind of banana that was pretty good. And *hola* means hello!"

As children of different cultures play and learn side by side, they gain an appreciation for their differences and an understanding of what unites them. Our greatest hope for ridding our society of racism, intolerance, and mistrust is when programs like these are reinforced in the home.

Father Francisco Gonzalez, Coordinator for Hispanic Family Life Ministry in the Archdiocese of Washington, told me about the struggles that many Hispanic families face when they first arrive in the United States. Father Gonzales said, "It is the story of every immigrant culture. There is a change in the whole structure of the family. The children have the better opportunity to learn the language through programs at their school. They are learning a language and being exposed to a culture that's different from their parents and grandparents. The children are often the link with the outside world. Inside the family, the roles of parent and child are firmly established, but outside the family the roles of parent and child are sometimes reversed. As a result, security does not always exist for family members as it had in the past."

The Alvarez family has been a gentle reminder to me that there are times in all our lives when we need to draw back the curtains and open the doors of our hearts and our homes to the newcomers in our midst. To live the gospel is to believe that when we welcome the stranger, we are welcoming Jesus.

Father Gonzales said, "The Church has a unique responsibility to combine the spiritual care of the Hispanic family with their basic needs to feel welcomed, to find a job, to settle in a home, and to receive an education. In the eyes of God we are all the same. God did not create any borders. He placed the earth in the hands of people from all cultures to work together to build up the kingdom of God."

Books You Can Read with Your Children

Elmer
by David McKee

The Berenstain Bears' New Neighbors
by Stan and Jan Berenstain

Masai and I
by Virginia Kroll

This Is Our House
by Michael Rosen

My Fellow Americans
by Alice Provensen

Straight to the Heart—Children of the World
by Ethan Hubbard

Grandfather's Journey
by Allen Say

Whoever You Are
by Mem Fox

In America
by Marissa Moss

Felita
by Nicholasa Mohr

Children Just Like Me
by Barnabas and Anabel Kindersley

Conversation Starters

1. If you had to move to a foreign land, what country would you choose? How would it feel to be a country where you didn't speak the language?

2. Were Mary and Joseph immigrants when they journeyed to Bethlehem? How were they treated?

Prayer

Lord Jesus, you know how it feels to be the outsider in a strange land. Help us to remember that when we welcome the stranger, we are welcoming you. Rid us of all fear and ignorance and enable us to see the many ways that people from different lands can enrich our lives. Move us outside our safe circles of friends and family, and remind us that we are all brothers and sisters in you. Amen.

The Third Week of September

A Family of Friends

"For an entire year I don't think I spoke more than thirty words; all I thought about was death," my friend Jeanne told me during a reunion of some of my closest college friends a few summers ago. "My doctor told me he had only cured the kind of cancer I had one other time."

I met Jeanne in 1976 during my freshman year in college. She was a prankster who loved to laugh and she made sure that everyone joined in with her. I often thought she missed her calling as a stand-up comedienne. After graduation Jeanne moved back to New York and I went to Washington, D.C. A few years later, an annual Christmas card became our way of keeping in touch. And then in 1989, just nine days before her thirtieth birthday, Jeanne was diagnosed with a malignancy in her abdomen. At times during her illness, Jeanne could even laugh about death.

At one point during her hospitalization her white blood cell count went down to zero. There was nothing in her body to fight off an infection. A cold could have killed her, so she was moved to isolation. "Picture this, " Jeanne said. "The doctors tell me I'm dying and 'oh, by the way, we're going to put you in a room by yourself for the next seven days!'"

Jeanne confided in me, "I honestly don't think I would have made it without the love and support of my friends and family. I never realized how much love there was in my life. I had friends who camped out in my hospital room. Neighbors who barely knew me often asked how I was doing. A group of grammar school friends took me out to dinner every time I was scheduled for chemotherapy. With that kind of support behind me, I stopped planning my funeral and started planning my five-year remission party."

In God's Words

Faithful friends are a sturdy shelter: whoever finds one has found a treasure. Faithful friends are beyond price; no amount can balance their worth. Faithful friends are life-saving medicine; and those who fear the Lord will find them.

— Sirach 6:14-16

Some friends play at friendship but a true friend sticks closer than one's nearest kin.

— Proverbs 18:24

"You are my friends if you do what I command you. I do not call you servants any longer, because the servant does not know what the master is doing; but I have called you friends, because I have made known to you everything that I have heard from my Father."

— John 15:14-15

What Can a Family Do?

1. Talk with your children about their friends. Get to know their friends by inviting them over to your home or out to the movies, etc.

2. When your children disagree with their friends, help them to see that friends can disagree and still be friends. It's a part of friendship.

3. Show your kids how to be a good friend. Stay in touch with your old friends whenever possible, even if it's once a year.

4. If one of your child's friends moves away, encourage him or her to keep in touch through cards, letters, e-mail, and an occasional phone call.

"It's been four and a half years and the cancer hasn't returned," Jeanne remarked proudly. "But every six months when I go for my complete CAT scan, the fears all come back. They're always there, just a quarter-inch below the surface. But I know I have friends and family who will help me through it."

Although I had seen Jeanne during her illness, I felt privileged to listen to her as she reflected so openly on a time of great suffering and despair in her life. And I thought how fortunate we both were that weekend to be part of a gathering of ten close friends whom we had known for more than fifteen years. For an entire weekend we put the demands of family, work, and other commitments on hold and we focused on friendship. Of course, we spent most of the weekend talking about our families and passing around photo albums.

It's a challenge to keep in touch with old friends as life hurries us along. Distance, misunderstandings, a hurt that never healed, or just the different paths of life can test even the most solid of friendships. As many of us start our own families, we realize how much time we each need to give to our spouse and children. But with all the pressures, worries, illnesses, and crises that families are facing, it seems we could all use a best friend now more than ever.

Sometimes it's important to let the yard work go, leave the office before dusk, put the kids to bed early, put down the good book you're reading, or pick up the phone. Better yet, find a blank note card and let a good friend know how much you care.

We should remember that Jesus knew what it meant to be a good friend. He listened to his friends; he calmed their fears, gave them encouragement, and believed in them. Jesus also spent a lot of time with his friends. He went fishing with his apostles and he enjoyed going over to Mary's and Martha's house for dinner. His friends were male and female; they were cowards, heroes, liars, cheaters, saints, and sinners. But he found goodness in all of them. And he didn't hold grudges. Not one of his closest friends could stay awake in his hour of need, but it was with these friends that he entrusted the mission of proclaiming the good news to people of all nations.

As I spent the weekend with my college friends, I thought about all the changes we had been through together. Whether it was over the phone or over a beer, a friend was always there to help, to comfort, to smile, or to hold. The words of these friends during the joys and sorrows of their lives are forever in my heart: "Harry and I are getting married in September!" "I lost my job." "I'm pregnant!" "My dad has pancreatic cancer." "It's a boy!" "I've been accepted into nursing school!" "We're moving back East!" "It's a girl!" "Mund had a heart attack." "I got a promotion!" "I had a miscarriage." "Tom and I are getting married in November!" "Jeanne has cancer."

A few weeks after our reunion, Jeanne called at 8:15 in the morning to wish me a happy birthday. "Well how does it feel to be getting up there?" she teased. "Oh it's not at bad as I thought it would be, " I said. "Yeah, especially when you consider the alternative," Jeanne said. And we laughed and laughed.

Books You Can Read with Your Children

Do You Want to Be My Friend?
by Eric Carle

Best Friends for Frances
by Russell Hoban

Winnie the Pooh
by A. A. Milne

Frog and Toad Together (and all other books in this series)
by Arnold Lobel

Little Bear's Friend
by Else H. Minarik

Toot and Puddle
by Holly Hobbie

Best Friends Together Again
by Aliki

52 Special Traditions for Family and Friends (52 Deck Series)
by Lynn Gordon

Amigo Means Friend
by L. Everett

The Faithful Friend
by Robert D. San Souci

Books and Resources for Parents

Good Friends Are Hard to Find: Help Your Child Find, Make and Keep Friends
by Fred Frankel, Ph.D.

Conversation Starters

1. Who are some of your best friends? How did you become friends? What are some of the things that make for a good friend?

2. Is Jesus your friend? What are some of the ways Jesus lets you know he's your friend?

Prayer

Dear Jesus, you taught us how to be a good friend and you showed us the importance of true friendship in our lives. You know how wonderful it feels to share meals, tell a joke, open our hearts, and relax with our closest friends. You also know how it feels when a friend lets you down. But your words and actions remind us of the need for acceptance, forgiveness, encouragement, and love with all our friends. Help us to recognize that the best friend we will ever have is you. At any hour of the day or night, you are always there to listen, to comfort, and to love us for who we are. Thank you for the gift of friends in our lives. Amen.

The Fourth Week of September

"The Beltway Prayer"

As the Powell family van entered the Beltway—a 63-mile maddening and sometimes treacherous stretch of highway circling the Washington metropolitan area—my friend Fran clutched the steering wheel tightly and asked her three small children, "Okay, who would like to say the 'Beltway Prayer?'"

On this outing, six-year-old Will led this original family prayer which is recited each time their van sets its wheels on the Beltway: "Dear Lord, please help Mom to be a safe driver. Let her be kind and courteous to the other drivers on the road. Please help us to behave ourselves and keep us from arguing so Mom can concentrate on her driving. Please make sure that the other drivers watch what they're doing. And bring us safely to our home. Amen."

We can often learn a lot from other families about finding creative ways to pray together. Fran, her husband, Bill, and their three children pray regularly as a family in the mornings and evenings, but they also turn to God at times throughout the day asking for help, guidance, or simply to say "good morning," "thank you," or "I'm sorry."

"Our family prayer was born in desperation," said Fran. "It seemed I could never find enough time to pray with three small children and the personal struggles, demands, and juggling acts we all have in life. For a while I would pray silently and then the kids would ask, 'Mom what are you doing?' And then I thought, 'Why don't I include them? It's so important for the kids to see that the strength I have comes from God. And that if I get upset or worried, I turn to God for help.'"

Many of us tend to compartmentalize our family prayer. It's dinner time—let's say grace. It's time for bed—don't forget to say your prayers. It's

In God's Words

"And whenever you pray, do not be like the hypocrites; for they love to stand and pray in the synagogues and at the street corners, so that they may be seen by others. . . . When you are praying, do not heap up empty phrases as the Gentiles do; for they think that they will be heard because of their many words. Do not be like them, for your Father knows what you need before you ask him."

— Matthew 6:5-8

"Whatever you ask for in prayer with faith, you will receive."

— Matthew 21:22

Rejoice in hope, be patient in suffering, persevere in prayer.

— Romans 12:12

Devote yourselves to prayer, keeping alert in it with thanksgiving.

— Colossians 4:2

What Can a Family Do?

1. Find a special time each day to pray together as a family.

2. Invite your children to write or collect their own prayers.

3. Teach your children traditional prayers, but also encourage them to create prayers of thanks or prayers for needs of others from their hearts.

4. Place your family Bible in a special place in your home. Read it often and treat the Bible with reverence.

5. Bring out the paints and markers and invite your children to draw their prayers or favorite story from the Bible.

6. Adapt "The Beltway Prayer" for your local highway before taking a family trip.

Sunday; time to go to church. Parents, religious educators, and priests all seem to agree that the evening meal should be a time of prayer and conversation for all families. I am hoping that they are referring to families whose children have reached the age of reason. If not, my family is in serious trouble.

When supper is served in our home, my son, Bobby, surveys his dinner plate and begins using negotiating skills that rival the Secretary of State's. "How about I eat four pieces of chicken and two carrots and then I get some vanilla ice cream?" My daughter, Teresa, who gives new meaning to the phrase inhale your food, is usually finished with her food (or she is wearing it) by the time grace is said. My prayer before dinner is that we will make it through the meal in once piece.

While we strive to establish regular times for prayer, the most important lesson we can teach our young children is that God is a part of everything we do and that we can pray to him whenever we want to.

In her inspiring and instructive book *And the Children Pray*, Janaan Manternach offers moving reflections and practical suggestions on helping children pray. It is a wonderful resource for families seeking to deepen their prayer life through both traditional prayers and activities that children enjoy, such as storytelling, music, writing, and art.

Dr. Manternach writes: "Prayer and church were always central to my family's lifestyle. God was blessed and thanked for any and all of the good things that happened in our lives. When we were worried, anxious, or afraid, we placed the situation in God's care. If some thing of beauty made us catch our breath, we uttered a prayer of praise. I believe this attitude is mostly acquired. And, the earlier children are put in touch with the presence of God in all things, especially people, and learn that God is present and acting in all events, the surer we can be that it will be a part of who and what they are."

Another marvelous resource for parents looking for ways to pray together as a family is *Catholic Household Blessings and Prayers*, published by the

National Conference of Catholic Bishops. The book includes traditional prayers along with blessings for families on birthdays, anniversaries, and days and seasons of the year. It also includes blessings before and after the birth of a child, blessings for families in times of trouble, and a blessing before a child leaves for school each morning.

The Bishops write: "Begin to pray beside your children even when they are very young. Pray in your own words, by all means, but pray especially the words of the church. Pray because you yourself need to pray. Then, as your children grow, invite them into this prayer. Bless them each night. Pray at table with them each evening. Let them hear you singing the songs of faith and reading the holy scriptures."

And to all those families who live in Washington or who come for a visit, I think the Bishops might add, "Don't forget to pray the Beltway Prayer." As six-year-old Will can tell you, it might just work a small miracle.

Books You Can Read with Your Children

Any Children's Bible

A Little Book of Poems and Prayers
by Joan Walsh Anglund

David and I Talk to God: Psalms for Children (series)
by Elspeth Campbell Murphy

God's Words in My Heart (series)
Elspeth Campbell Murphy

A Child's Book of Celtic Prayers
by Joyce Denham

God in Between
by Sandy Eisenberg Sasso

My First Book of Prayers (Precious Moments)
by Daniel J. Porter

God of My Heart: A Prayer Book for Youth (Teens)
edited by Connie Wlaschin Ruhlman

Books and Resources for Parents

And the Children Pray
by Janaan Manternach with Carl J. Pfeifer

Family Prayer for Family Times
by Kathleen O'Connell Chesto

Family Spirituality
by Kathleen O'Connell Chesto

In My Heart Room (Books I and II)
by Mary Terese Donze, A.P.S.

Guided Meditations
by Jane Reehorst, B.V.M.

Pathways to Praying with Teens
by Maryann Hakowski

The Logic of Happiness: Proverbs and Practical Wisdom for Spiritual Living
by Philip St. Romain

Let's Say Grace: Mealtime Prayers for Family Occasions Throughout the Year
by Robert Hamma

Conversation Starters

1. What is prayer? To me, prayer is . . .

2. It's important to talk to God because . . .

Prayer

The Lord's Prayer

"Pray then in this way:
Our Father, who art in heaven,
hallowed be thy name;
they kingdom come;
thy will be done on earth as it is in heaven.
Give us this day our daily bread;
and forgive us our trespasses
as we forgive those who trespass against us;
and lead us not into temptation, but deliver us from evil.
Amen."

The First Week of October

All Good Gifts

My son, Bobby, sat at the kitchen table with paper and marker in hand and began studying the artwork taped to the wall that his cousin Patty had given him a few weeks earlier. Although she was barely three-and-one-half years old at the time, Patty had written all the letters of Bobby's name and then topped off her masterpiece with blue glitter and a hot-pink snowflake sticker.

Bobby, who was four years old at the time, looked at me and with great frustration said, "I can't make letters like Patty; I can only make mountains." I glanced over at his orange and brown drawing and said, "Oh, but you make such nice mountains. Did you know that every kid has special things that they can do? God gives every child a special gift or talent. And the nicest part of having a talent is that you can share what you're able to do with other kids. Patty shows you how to use her glitter and glue and you show her how to swing a baseball bat."

"Mom, I told you, I can only make mountains!" Bobby said. So much for my parental words of wisdom.

At an early age, children understand that there are some things in life that come easy to them and other things that they will struggle with. It's critical to a child's development to discover which activities bring them joy and satisfaction. But it seems that there is a tremendous amount of pressure on young children today to exhibit their talents and "show their stuff" to a society that rewards the achievers and ignores all others.

Many parents feel this pressure and respond in a variety of ways. Some parents enroll their children in more activities than a child can possibly handle. I know of a dad who is a frustrated athlete and a mom whose modeling career never quite took off.

In God's Words

Pursue love and strive for the spiritual gifts.

— 1 Corinthians 14:1

To one is given through the Spirit the utterance of wisdom, and to another the utterance of knowledge according to the same Spirit, to another faith by the same Spirit, to another gifts of healing by the one Spirit, to another the working of miracles, to another prophecy, to another the discernment of spirits, to another various kinds of tongues, to another the interpretation of tongues. All these are activated by one and the same Spirit, who allots to each one individually just as the Spirit chooses.

— 1 Corinthians 12:8-11

What Can a Family Do?

1. Light seven candles at your dinner table and explain to your children the seven gifts of the Holy Spirit: wisdom, understanding, right judgment, courage, knowledge, reverence, and wonder. Nurture these spiritual gifts in your children.

2. Bless your children each evening and say a prayer thanking God for a special gift that they used that day, e.g., patience, kindness, perseverance, etc.

3. If you have more than one child, invite your children to say something special that their brother or sister did during the week that showed love, patience, forgiveness, kindness, or honesty.

4. Celebrate your child's unique abilities; avoid comparing your child's talents to others.

Their children are programmed to fulfill their parents' unfinished dreams rather than pursue their own. Other parents seek to encourage their children in their endeavors and provide the right amount of opportunities for their children's talents to flourish.

As parents, we enjoy taking pride in our children's accomplishments. And when we see even a hint of a talent or skill, it's only natural to put our lives on fast-forward and see our children batting in the final game of the World Series, performing in the National Symphony Orchestra or accepting the Nobel Peace Prize. It's just as natural to find ourselves comparing another child's abilities with our own child's, as much as we wish we didn't fall into this trap.

A lot of time and energy are devoted to activities that bring our children enjoyment and recognition for their skills. As we juggle our schedules for soccer games, dance recitals, baseball practice, piano lessons, or scout meetings, one of the most important activities we need to schedule is time with mom and dad. According to *The Washington Post*, a University of Maryland study found that parents spend approximately two hours a day with their children, and today's average working dad converses less than eight minutes a day with his children, four minutes if his wife also works outside the home. In the hurried lives of today's busy parents, we sometimes forget that what our children need and want most is our time.

In a society that is preoccupied with gifted students and record-breaking test scores, it's important to remember that we hold the key to the more important gifts of kindness, patience, love, wisdom, sensitivity, and faith. My friend Fran recently told me, "When I pray at night with my children, I thank God for Will's kindness to other children, for Jilly's strength of character, and for Elliot's cooperation during the day. The kids need to see that I recognize their wonderful gifts. Together we thank God for all that he has given us."

We need to teach our children that any talent or skill that they have is a gift from God. We have a responsibility to use these precious gifts in a way that is pleasing to God and that helps the human family. St. Paul writes eloquently about the spiritual gifts we have received: "Now there are varieties of gifts, but the same Spirit; and there are varieties of services, but the same Lord; and there are varieties of activities, but it is the same God who activates all of them in everyone. To each is given the manifestation of the Spirit for the common good" (1 Corinthians 12:4-7).

I thank God for blessing my family and friends with so many gifts. But it often disturbs me to think of the millions of children who are denied an opportunity to develop their gifts because they are too busy searching for food and shelter, dodging bullets in their apartment complex, steering clear of drug pushers on the playground, or running from abusive parents who should be protecting them and nurturing their gifts.

I know of many men and women professionals and college and high school students who volunteer as tutors, mentors, coaches, or Big Brothers and Big Sisters as a way of thanking God for all the blessings he has given them. These are all ways of showing how we can join together to use our gifts to build a more just and caring community for all children.

A few weeks after Patty had given Bobby her artwork, Bobby called excitedly from the kitchen, "I made an X! I made an X! Mommy, come see!" Sure enough, next to his mountain range was a real live X. "Tomorrow, I will make a B like Patty does," he announced.

With the right amount of love and encouragement from parents, and the belief that all good gifts come from God, our children will learn to create their own masterpieces. They may even find the faith in themselves to make and to move mountains.

Books You Can Read with Your Children

The Art Lesson
by Tomie dePaola

Matthew's Dream
by Leo Lionni

Everyone Is Good for Something
by Beatrice Schenk de Regniers

Amazing Grace
by Mary Hoffman

Gifted Kids Speak Out: Hundreds of Kids Ages 6-13 Talk About School, Friends, Their Families and the Future
by James R. Delisle, Ph.D.

Have You Ever Seen an Elephant Sneeze?
by Bernadette McCarver Snyder

Have You Ever Heard a Hummingbird Hum?
by Bernadette McCarver Snyder

Have You Ever Heard a Catfish Purr?
by Bernadette McCarver Snyder

Books and Resources for Parents

The Survival Guide for Parents of Gifted Kids: How to Understand, Live With, and Stick Up for Your Gifted Child
by Sally Yahnke Walker

Gift From the Sea
by Anne Morrow Lindbergh

The Hurried Child
by David Elkind

Little Man Tate (Videotape)
from Orion Pictures

Searching for Bobby Fischer (Videotape) from Paramount Studios

Conversation Starters

1. Do you have a special talent or something you like to do?

2. How can you use this talent to show God's love to others?

Prayer

Generous God, giver of all good gifts, thank you for our children's skills and accomplishments. May we never lose sight that these gifts come from you. Teach us to value not only those gifts recognized by our society, but the simple gifts like faith, patience, generosity, or kindness. Help us to see that the truly gifted and talented children are those who use their abilities to bring people closer to you. We ask this through Christ our Lord. Amen.

The Second Week of October

Bullies and the Bible

My friend's son got off the school bus and was terribly upset. A "mean kid" on the bus had been making fun of the size of Will's ears in front of all the children. When Will's younger sister heard this, she told the instigator to "cut it out." The "mean kid" turned to her and called her "skinny bones" and "bean pole."

I remember thinking how cruel children can be to one another. Will, the eldest son of one of my closest friends, is a popular, friendly, caring, and intelligent boy. What would cause another child to want to hurt someone who is always so kind?

When my son, Bobby, was in kindergarten, I received a call one day from the school nurse. Bobby had been complaining of a headache and a stomachache. But when I arrived at school I discovered that the real cause of Bobby's malady was a fellow kindergartner who was bullying him in the lunch room.

For me, and I suspect for many other parents, all the wonderful wisdom of "turning the other cheek," "loving our enemies," and "blessed are the peacemakers" goes right out the window when one of my children is intentionally hurt or threatened by another child. Fortunately, these feelings are only fleeting because some of the most important lessons we teach our children involve forgiving people who have hurt them.

My husband, Joe, and I have always taught our children to use their words instead of their fists unless it's to protect themselves. When other children have repeatedly hurt or threatened them or their friends, we have explained that the reason a kid usually does something bad to another kid is because he doesn't feel very good about himself or has not learned how to respect other people.

In God's Words

And there came out from the camp of the Philistines a champion named Goliath, of Gath, whose height was six cubits and a span.

— 1 Samuel 17:4

Guard me, O Lord, from the hands of the wicked; protect me from the violent who have planned my downfall.

— Psalm 140:4-5

And they clothed him in a purple cloak; and after twisting some thorns into a crown, they put it on him. And they began saluting him, "Hail, King of the Jews!" They struck his head with a reed, spat upon him, and knelt down in homage to him. After mocking him, they stripped him of the purple cloak and put his own clothes on him. Then they led him out to crucify him.

— Mark 15:17-20

What Can a Family Do?

1. Refuse to tolerate hateful attitudes or ethnic jokes in your own home or anywhere else.

2. Write a letter or pick up the telephone to protest federal, state, or local legislation that undermines human life or human dignity.

3. Look for examples of racism, sexism, or religious stereotypes when watching TV with your kids and discuss them. Talk about how these attitudes contribute to feelings of superiority and arrogance.

4. Read the story of David and Goliath (1 Samuel 17), Moses and the Pharaoh (Exodus 3-14), and Jesus and Pilate (Matthew 27:11-26, Mark 15:1-15, Luke 23:1-25, or John 18:28-19:16) with your children. Who is the bully in each story and how do the others respond?

We ask our children not to spend time figuring out the reasons for the slight, but to make sure they always try to work out their problems peacefully. We try not to use the word "bully" when we're talking about a child we know. As angry as a child's actions can make us, it's usually not their fault, and labeling a child as a troublemaker only makes things worse for the child. In the book *The Berenstain Bears and the Bully*, we're reminded that a "bully" often has a mother or father who "bullies" him or her and they need special understanding.

There are lots of reasons why children can be cruel to other children: emotional and physiological problems, stressful events in the home, some stages of child development bring about changes in a child's behavior. Every child has his moments, but it's the repeated ridicule and put-downs, the persistent punching and shoving, the ceaseless name calling that can make life absolutely miserable for the child on the receiving end.

Some children use aggressive language out of fear—fear that someone looks different or acts differently. Children can also be cruel to other children because their parents have passed on religious, racial, or cultural prejudices to them. The children are mimicking what they see and hear in their homes. Children who act out of fear or prejudice have not been taught to recognize and respect the importance and uniqueness of all people.

I know that Will's and Bobby's encounters with troublemakers will certainly not be their last. Unfortunately it's a very unpleasant part of life for children as well as parents because we can't be there to referee for our kids; we can only coach from the sidelines. The stakes seem so much higher in the world our children are growing up in. Instead of sticks and stones, today's older bullies are using guns and knives.

I told Bobby that he couldn't run away from his problem with the troublemaker at school or else this classmate would always bother him. Joe and I talked with him about the times we had to deal with bullies in our lives as children and as adults. And then we reminded him that he could use the "DeBug Program" that he learned in his kindergarten in Maryland.

DeBug is a wonderful program adopted by the Montgomery County Public Schools in Maryland. The purpose of DeBug is to equip children with a series of steps in which they learn to solve problems when others are "bugging" them. It helps children learn to be assertive and, when possible, to resolve the difficulty themselves. The five steps of the DeBug system are simple. The children are taught that if someone is bugging them, they should try the following: 1. IGNORE. If that doesn't work . . . 2. MOVE AWAY. If that doesn't work . . . 3. TALK FRIENDLY. If that doesn't work . . . 4. TALK FIRMLY. If that doesn't work . . . 5. GET ADULT HELP.

As Christians, we recognize that all people are deserving of love and respect. The cause of many of the problems in our world is that people are not treated with respect and dignity. The expressions of other cultures and religions may be very different from our own, but all people are called to glory. Every person is a child of God. When we put down other religions, or show disrespect to an immigrant family or fall into cultural or religious stereotypes, we become the bully who feels better about himself by putting other people down. We need to remember the words of Jesus in Matthew's Gospel: "Do to others as you would have them do to you" (Matthew 7:12). Or, as I often tell my own children, "Treat other people the way you want to be treated." The words that usually make the most sense to my kids are: "How would that make you feel if someone said or did that to you?"

Interestingly, the Bible is filled with bullies: kings and armies who invaded lands that weren't theirs, Pharaohs who persecuted and oppressed the less powerful, and cruel leaders who tortured entire cities of people. But the commandment "Love your enemies and pray for those who persecute you" is the way Jesus asks us to respond to the cruelties others bring against us. It's the only lasting way to get rid of the darkness and hatred in our world.

Books You Can Read with Your Children

The Berenstain Bears and the Bully
by Stan and Jan Berenstain

Bullies Are a Pain in the Brain
by Trevor Romain

Yertle the Turtle and Other Stories
by Dr. Seuss

How the Grinch Stole Christmas
by Dr. Seuss

Tyrone the Horrible
by Hans Wilhelm

Cliques, Phonies, and Other Baloney
by Trevor Romain

The Grouchy Ladybug
by Eric Carle

The Meanest Thing to Say
by Bill Cosby

We Can Get Along: A Child's Book of Choices
by Lauren Murphy Payne, M.S.W.

Stick Up for Yourself: Every Kid's Guide to Personal Power and Positive Self-Esteem (Ages 8-12)
by Gershen Kaufman, Ph.D., and Lev Raphael, Ph.D.

The Bully of Barkham Street
by Mary Stolz (Grades 3-6)

The Ears of Louis
by Constance C. Greene (Grades 3-5)

Books and Resources for Parents

What to Do When Kids Are Mean to Your Child: Real Solutions from Parents, Experts and Kids
by Elin McCoy

Good Friends Are Hard to Find: Help Your Child Find, Make and Keep Friends
by Fred Frankel, Ph.D.

Respecting Our Differences: A Guide to Getting Along in a Changing World (Ages 13 & up)
by Lynn Duvall

The Bully-Free Classroom: Over 100 Tips and Strategies for Teachers K-12
by Allan Beane, Ph.D.

Conversation Starters

1. Have you ever been teased or bullied? How did you feel? What did you do about it?

2. What do you think it means to "turn the other cheek?"

Jesus experienced firsthand how challenging this commandment could be. He suffered humiliation and agony at the hands of his tormentors. Soldiers mocked and ridiculed him with a crown of thorns and a scarlet cloak. Jesus was blindfolded, slapped, and beaten. He was jeered by a crowd and taunted by scribes and elders. He was led to a degrading death and still the insults kept coming. But as he hung on the cross Jesus prayed, "Father forgive them; for they do not know what they are doing" (Luke 23:34).

Prayer

Dear Jesus, you know what it feels like to be teased and bullied. Help us to remember that no matter how mean others might treat us, or how much we might suffer from their cruelties, we will never be alone, for you are standing by us. Fill us with your courage, dignity, forgiveness, and faith as we meet difficult people. We pray for them, too, that they will find peace with themselves. We ask this through Christ our Lord. Amen.

The Third Week of October

Sisters and Brothers

"The doctor couldn't get a clear picture on the mammogram," my sister Nancy told me during a phone conversation a few years ago. "She just said there is some type of mass and they aren't sure what it is, so they're going to take another mammogram in a few days."

I tried to tell myself that everything would work out fine for Nancy. It's not uncommon for many women to be called back for a second mammogram. Still, I was having some trouble dismissing the thought that both my great-grandmother and grandmother had suffered from breast cancer. Nancy tried to keep an optimistic attitude especially as she thought about her husband and two children. But while drinking her morning coffee she had picked up the paper and read a Peanuts cartoon. Charlie Brown says, "Sometimes I lie awake at night and I ask, 'Why me?'" Then a voice answers: "Nothing personal. Your name just happened to come up." Nancy said, "I thought, what if this time my name just happened to come up?"

A while later I hung up the phone with Nancy and between a few tears I asked God to take care of my big sister. Like most brothers and sisters, we are different in so many ways, but we are the same where it really matters. We understand on the deepest level that a sister or brother is one of the most precious gifts we receive from God.

By the end of the week Nancy had received the good news that there was nothing to worry about and no further tests were needed. But during the four days that we waited for Nancy's results, my husband, Joe, and I spent a lot of time talking about the special relationship we have with each of our sisters and brothers and how much richer our lives are because they are here.

In God's Words

"But I say to you that if you are angry with a brother or sister, you will be liable to judgment, and if you insult a brother or sister, you will be liable to the council."

— Matthew 5:22

Those who say, "I love God," and hate their brothers or sisters, are liars; for those who do not love a brother or sister whom they have seen, cannot love God whom they have not seen. The commandment we have from him is this: those who love God must love their brothers and sisters also.

— 1 John 4:20-21

What Can a Family Do?

1. Remember to compliment your children when you see they are being kind or caring toward each other, e.g., "It was really nice how you helped your sister up after she fell down at the playground."

2. Ask your children to apologize whenever they physically or emotionally hurt one another.

3. Nurture the relationship between your siblings whenever you can. Many of my friends tell their kids, "Friends may come and go but your brother or sister will be there forever."

4. Set good examples with your siblings no matter how close or faraway they live from you. Stay in touch, apologize if you have a disagreement, and arrange family reunions whenever it's possible or on special occasions.

5. Read the story of Cain and Abel (Genesis 4:1-16) and Joseph and his brothers (Genesis 37). What led some of the brothers to behave so poorly?

For forty years, Nancy and I have been blessed to share a very close and loving relationship. The night Nancy left for college, I cried all night. Not only would I miss her terribly, I was the one left behind with four younger brothers! Although Nancy and I are only fourteen months apart, my mother has told us that we rarely fought as kids. And except for the time that Nancy "trimmed" my hair in high school and the time I told her how much I "disliked" her boyfriend in college, I can't remember any major disagreement between us.

What I do remember are the many nights we stayed up late watching old movies together as we talked about school, our hopes, our dreams, friends, and boys. We served as maid of honor in each other's weddings. And as godmothers we promised to help raise each other's children in the faith of our church.

As I thought about my sister, I realized the importance of fostering a relationship between my own son and daughter. As parents we have a tremendous responsibility and challenge to teach our children respect and concern for one another. But as any parent with young children will tell you, this is easier said than done.

"I don't like Teresa today; she is bothering me!" announced my four-year-old son, Bobby, during one of the days that we waited for Nancy's results. Teresa knew on some level that an unkind remark had been lobbed her way. She responded like most two-year-olds do: she crossed her eyes and let out a series of grunts that in seconds escalated to a rhinoceros pitch. But a few days later I actually saw Bobby helping Teresa take off her coat and boots after a romp in the snow. And one night before bed time later that week, I heard Bobby "reading" *Go Dog Go!* to her. There is still hope.

Somewhere between the grunts and groans, the bickering and the needling, the laughter and the tenderness, relationships are forming in the early years of our children's lives that will forever join their hearts. Sometimes these hearts are broken by jealousy, an unkind remark, a long-standing feud or an inability to understand each other. But God lets us know that although the pain and hurt are very real, it's more important to have forgiveness and peace rather than anger and discord in our families.

In many families, the unique bond of love and loyalty between siblings is what enables brothers and sisters to help each other through some of life's most difficult struggles. It is this compassion, love, and closeness that Jesus would like us to emulate when he invites us to be brothers and sisters in Christ. But God does not only ask us to follow this example in our immediate families. Through the Gospel of Matthew we are reminded that a homeless woman, a poor child, a hungry family, a lonely prisoner, are all our brothers and sisters. When we reach out to them, we are reaching out to God and helping the entire human family. St. Mark tells us, "Whoever does the will of God is my brother and sister and mother" (3:35).

A few days after Nancy got the good news from her doctor, she wrote me a note: "Thanks for worrying so much about me. I can't tell you how much it helped to have someone to share my fears with. After the initial shock and terror, I felt a kind of acceptance. There was nothing I could do to change what was or wasn't there. I would just take it one step at a time. Thankfully, this time there was only one step to take. But the love and support of family helped tremendously. I'm very fortunate to have you as my sister. God has been very good to me." He's been very good to me too, Nancy.

Books You Can Read with Your Children

The Pain and the Great One
by Judy Blume

My Rotten Redheaded Older Brother
by Patricia Polacco

The Lapsnatcher
by Bruce Coville

Julius: the Baby of the World
by Kevin Henkes

Living with a Brother or Sister With Special Needs: A Book for Sibs
by Donald Meyer and Patricia Vadasy

Will I Ever Be Older
by Eva H. Grant

Nobody Ever Asked Me If I Wanted A Baby Sister
by Martha Alexander

Brothers
by Florence B. Freedman

Books and Resources for Parents

Siblings Without Rivalry
by Adele Faber and Elaine Mazlish

Sisters
by Carol Saline

Conversation Starters

1. What makes your brother(s) or sister(s) special to you?

2. What do you think Jesus means when he says that we are all brothers and sisters? Is this hard for you to imagine?

Prayer

Dear God, thank you for the gift of our brothers and sisters and for blessing the love between us in a special way. As we go through life's joys and sorrows, holidays and heartaches, births and deaths together, strengthen the bonds of love so that they will never be broken. Help us to extend this love and to see all people as our brothers and sisters, especially those who are poor, homeless, imprisoned, or sick. Help us to remember that when we reach out to them we are reaching out to you. Amen.

The Fourth Week of October

Halloween is celebrated on October 31.

Fear

"But I don't want to go to school," cried five-year-old Marisa on the morning of her first day of kindergarten. "I'm afraid I won't be able to find my classroom by myself and I don't want to be at school that long," she sobbed. Marisa is a lovely child who is usually pleasant and cooperative. But on this particular morning she was out of sorts. Her long dark curls weren't even close to being combed as she pleaded with her mother in a frightened voice to let her stay home.

"From the moment she got up in the morning it started," said her mother Christine. "She would beg me not to make her go to school because she didn't want to be away from home. She wanted to know what I was doing when she was at school and if I would I always be there to meet her when school was over. Every day was such a struggle that by the time we got to the bus stop we were both emotionally drained. And then I knew we'd be going through the same thing all over again the next day."

At school, things weren't any easier for Marisa. She was promised she could call home if she stopped crying. When she called, Christine listened to Marisa struggling for breath as she tried to compose herself long enough to be reassured by her mother's loving and gentle voice. One night Marisa said to her mother and father, "Do you know what the very worst part is about going to school? Well, it's when I'm getting ready to cry and all the kids say, 'Oh no, not again!'"

My friend Christine had called me when Marisa's fear of school continued because she remembered that my son Bobby had a similar reaction during his first weeks of pre-school. I dreaded Mondays and Wednesdays because it meant a morning of tears as Bobby was being pried off my

In God's Words

I put my trust in you. In God, whose word I praise, in God I trust; I am not afraid.

— Psalm 56:3-4

Do not fear, for I am with you, do not be afraid, for I am your God; I will strengthen you, I will help you, I will uphold you with my victorious right hand.

— Isaiah 41:10

"Peace I leave with you; my peace I give to you. I do not give to you as the world gives. Do not let your hearts be troubled, and do not let them be afraid."

— John 14:27

What Can a Family Do?

1. Talk to your children openly and honestly about their fears. Read stories and talk about ways that children and adults face their fears.

2. Let your children know that when they're afraid, they can pray and give their worries to God. Give your child a special blessing at his or her bedtime when they are worried or frightened.

3. Remind your children that adults have fears too. Share stories of things that you were afraid of when you were their age.

4. Did you know that Michael Jordan has hydrophobia (fear of water) and won't go in deep water? Olympic gymnast Amy Chow has a terrible fear of spiders? Gold medalist Mia Hamm of the U.S. Women's National Soccer Team is afraid to watch a scary movie? Baseball slugger Bobby Bonilla hates to fly? And Patrick Ewing of the New York Knicks was terribly frightened of ghosts when he was a child? (Source: *Sports Illustrated for Kids*, Fall 1997) It's important to tell your children that everyone—even athletes and people they look up to—have had to face their fears too.

knee by a teacher and a teacher's aide. I cried my own tears outside the classroom door until I heard his sobs gradually turn to whimpers. But I told Christine that Bobby's fears soon passed. A few weeks after the crying episodes, he told me that he loved his teacher, and that he had a new best friend named William.

Fears come in all shapes and sizes and children don't have a corner on the market. As adults, we often have a difficult time coming face to face with our own fears. I think that's one of the reasons our children's fears can upset us on such a deep level; we still know what it's like to be afraid. When a child wakes up frightened during a nightmare or a thunderstorm, we hold her tightly, hoping to shield her from all of life's bad dreams. As adults and parents, we know that a warm hug will provide comfort, but it won't chase away the real darkness in our lives.

Too many parents and children are experiencing living nightmares every night and day. A mother living in poverty fears a storm of insensitivity as she is uncertain about how she will feed and shelter her children. A hard-working father worries about a real monster—losing his job. Many families are scared when the darkness of illness, natural disasters, prejudice, or injustice enters their lives. Other families live in the shadow of daily fear when a family member suffers from mental illness or depression.

How do parents living with such fear instill a sense of hope and promise in their children's lives? As parents, we have a responsibility to help our children work through their fears as we continue to confront our own. As God's people, we also have a responsibility to reach out to others who live in fear and sorrow because of injustice, illness, or hatred.

We may think that fear, anxiety, and panic are more common in today's world. But the Bible is filled with examples of people who understood fear and who knew disease, famine, war, and persecution. Even the apostles were gripped by fear. They denied knowing Jesus and hid from Jesus' enemies after his arrest because they were filled with fear and panic.

As we confront our own fears, it's very comforting to know that Jesus understood and felt fear on its deepest level on the night before he died. St. Luke writes that Jesus was so distressed in the Garden of Gethsemane, that "his sweat became like great drops of blood falling down on the ground" (22:44). But in his anguish and sorrow he turned to his Father and prayed, "Not my will but yours be done" (Luke 22:42).

St. Paul reminds us that only by turning our worries, fears, and concerns over to God, no matter how great or small, will we find true peace. "Do not worry about anything, but in everything by prayer and supplication with thanksgiving let your requests be made known to God. And the peace of God, which surpasses all understanding, will guard your hearts and your minds in Christ Jesus" (Philippians 4:6-7).

My friend Christine understands the importance of prayer, especially when coming to terms with fear. She said to me, "I would pray on my way to the bus stop that everything was going okay for Marisa. I prayed while I was making lunch for my other two children, and I prayed while I sat there wondering if Marisa and her teacher would need to call home again. It might sound funny but it seemed like prayer was not only my connection with God but also with Marisa when she wasn't there."

"I think that prayer, time, and a nurturing teacher all helped Marisa," Christine said. "Last week Marisa's dad was a chaperone on the class trip to the zoo. When the trip was over, Marisa said, 'From now on, Dad, I don't think you and Mom need to be at school anymore.'"

Books You Can Read with Your Children

The Berenstain Bears and the Bad Dream
by Stan and Jan Berenstain

Where the Wild Things Are
by Maurice Sendak

There's a Monster Under My Bed
by James Howe

Life Doesn't Frighten Me
by Maya Angelou

The Knight Who Was Afraid of the Dark
by Barbara S. Hazen

Once When I Was Scared
by Helena C. Pittman

The Monster at the End of This Book, Starring Lovable, Furry Old Grover
by Jon Stone

Books and Resources for Parents

Let Go of Fear: Tackling Our Worst Emotion
by Carlos G. Valles

Protect Us from All Anxiety: Meditations for the Depressed
by William Burke

Conversation Starters

1. Talk about a time when you were afraid. What helped you to feel better about your fears?

2. Jesus tell us many times, "Do not be afraid." How do you think he wants us to handle our fears?

Prayer

Heavenly Father, you have told us to put our trust in you when we are anxious and afraid. It is not always easy to face our fears, but it helps to know that we can turn to you in these difficult times. Some days it seems that there are so many things to be frightened of in our world. Your words gently remind us to stop worrying; you will take care of us. When our friends, neighbors, and others are living through the real worries of illness, homelessness, and joblessness, help us to reach out to them and alleviate their fears and suffering. Give us your strength, your protection, and your peace as we face our fears. We ask this through Christ our Lord. Amen.

The First Week of November

November 1 is All Saints Day.

No Greater Love

In the autumn of 1996, on a golden afternoon, my daughter, Teresa, and I picked up my first grader, Bobby, in front of his elementary school.

About ten minutes after dismissal, a number of parents were still outside the school when a mother, arriving in front of the school to pick up her child, lost control of her minivan. The van jumped the curb a few feet from where we were standing and began driving through a crowd of parents, teachers, students, and the principal. I watched in horror as I saw my friend Maureen struck by the van. Seconds later, the school principal, Mr. Bricketto, was also struck and knocked to the ground as he was pushing children out of the minivan's path. I saw a woman take her child and throw her into the arms of another woman to keep her from getting hit. This mother was then struck and dragged underneath the van. A pine tree finally stopped the out-of-control van, pinning her underneath it. I couldn't tell from where I was standing if anyone else had been hit or pulled under the van.

When I saw that the van had stopped and that my children were safe, I ran over to Maureen who was pleading with me and my son's teacher to find her daughter, Christine, a classmate of my son's. I don't remember running over to the van, but by the time I got there, Mr. Bricketto was already there. The woman who had been dragged under the van couldn't be moved in case she had a spinal cord injury, so Mr. Bricketto steered and eased the van off of her as those of us there lifted up the back of the van. In absolute terror, I looked underneath the van praying to God that I would not see Christine's face or any child's alongside the injured woman—I then realized it was my friend, Nancy the mother of another first grader.

In God's Words

"Be strong and courageous, do not be frightened or dismayed, for the Lord your God is with you wherever you go."

— Joshua 1:9

That night the Lord stood near him and said, "Keep up your courage."

— Acts 23:11

We know love by this, that he laid down his life for us—and we ought to lay down our lives for one another.

— 1 John 3:16

What Can a Family Do?

1. Tell your children about a hero or saint who inspired you and made a difference in your life.

2. Read some stories of the saints and talk about the courage they needed to keep their faith or to speak out against injustice.

3. Who are the heroes in our society today? Are sports figures and entertainers our heroes? Should they be? What's the difference between a celebrity and a hero?

4. Talk with your children about heroes and saints. How are they similar? How are they different?

5. Can you think of a woman, a man, or a child that you know who has shown real courage?

As heart wrenching as it was to see Nancy, I was relieved there wasn't a child under the van. I was also relieved that there were three nurses on the scene—two were mothers who moments before were in the minivan's direct path. Now they were treating Nancy with extraordinary skill and compassion.

Meanwhile, the rest of us tried to make sense of what had just happened. We learned that the driver of the van lost control of her vehicle when she saw that her second grader was just about to slam the door on her four-year old daughter's hand. In her panic, she thought she was slamming her foot on the brake but her foot hit the gas pedal instead.

When the paramedics arrived, Nancy was air-lifted to a trauma intensive care unit where she remained in critical condition for ten days. Through prayer and Nancy's remarkably brave spirit, she was released from the hospital and received extensive physical therapy. Maureen was taken to a local hospital that afternoon where she was treated for two hip fractures. Mr. Bricketto finally agreed to have his shoulder x-rayed only after everyone else was taken care of on the day of the accident.

Following the accident, many of the neighborhood mothers and children who were at the accident scene gathered at our friend Maria's house so we could all be together. We prayed for everyone involved, especially for Nancy. And then we talked about how it could have easily been any one of us driving the van or getting hit by the van.

We've all had our days when we're the parent doing all the wrong things. The blood-curdling screams of our child in pain or fear can momentarily disconnect our thoughts from our actions. In our full and frenzied lives we're often balancing sanity and safety. While our right foot rests on the brake, our left foot impatiently taps as if somehow the red light will change faster or the kids will suddenly quiet down or the snarl of traffic will miraculously unravel. We want to believe that we're the perfect parent who never makes mistakes, who's always on time, and whose patience never runs out. But we know better.

Sometimes we can forget that we're also the parent doing all the right things. We're picking up our children from school and holding their hand as we ask about their day. We're following all the rules of safety and still the unthinkable happens.

In truth, most days we're a little of both kinds of parents. We're filled up with stress, commitments, and pressures, but we're also filled up with a love and a protective instinct for our children that runs so deep it can almost be terrifying. It's this love that caused one mother to protect her daughter as her hand was about to be caught in a door and another mother to save her daughter's life while risking her own. Our lives can be changed forever in seconds. And that can make our world seem as out of control as a runaway minivan.

The images of the accident were difficult to erase from my mind during the weeks that followed. But they were gradually replaced with the more powerful images of a community that reached out with love and kindness, with meals, babysitting, car pools, thoughts, and prayers.

The terrifying memory of children being pushed out of harm's way have taken on a more comforting meaning for me today. With true courage, Nancy risked her life to save the life of her daughter. Shortly after the accident someone asked me if I could ever feel that my son was safe at school again. I saw first-hand how our principal risked his life to save the lives of his students as if they were his own children. I'm certain there's no place on earth that my son is safer.

In years ahead, as Nancy, Maureen, and Mr. Bricketto struggle with emotional and physical pain, I hope they never lose sight of the gift of love and life they gave to the children on that autumn afternoon. In their most difficult hours, may they find comfort in the words Jesus spoke in the Gospel of John: "No one has greater love than this, to lay down one's life for one's friends" (15:13).

Books You Can Read with Your Children

The Children's Book of Heroes
edited by William J. Bennett

A Year with the Saints
by Mark Water

115 Saintly Fun Facts
by Bernadette McCarver Snyder

My Bedtime Book of the Saints
by Father Frank Lee, C.S.S.R.

Heroes
by Ken Mochizuki

Five Brave Explorers (Great Black Heroes)
by Wade Hudson

Frog Is a Hero
by Max Velthuijs

Hoop Heroes: Hardaway, Hill, Marbury, Ewing
by Sydelle Kramer

Can You Find Bible Heroes?
by Philip Gallery

The Brave Little Toaster
by Thomas M. Disch (Videotape from Disney)

Saint George and the Dragon
retold by Margaret Hodges

Little Tim and the Brave Sea Captain
by Edward Ardizzone

Thunder Cake
by Patricia Polacco

Conversation Starters

1. Do you have a hero? What is special about that person that makes him/her a hero to you?

2. Is a hero always a saint? What's the difference?

Prayer

Heavenly Father, the lives of the saints and of true heroes can overwhelm us. These women and men seem too good to be true. How can we ever measure up to them? Where do we find the courage and the love to lead such special lives? Help us remember that the saints and heroes were not perfect people; in many ways, they were people just like us. They made mistakes, they had their faults, and they experienced times of doubt and uncertainty. But through prayer they found the faith and courage to follow your will. Thank you for the saints we remember this week and for the many unsung saints and heroes who have touched our lives. May their example be a source of hope and promise for us all. We ask this through Christ our Lord. Amen.

The Second Week of November

November is the month to remember those who have died.

Heaven on Earth

A few years ago, as we traveled down the New Jersey Turnpike, my son, Bobby, who was four years old at the time, almost whispered from the back seat: "Is Grandma Kitty in heaven tonight?" "Yes," my husband, Joe, and I answered without hesitating. "Well," Bobby continued, "I don't ever want to go to heaven. I want to stay right here." And thirty seconds later, having said his piece, he fell soundly asleep.

That day had been difficult for Bobby and for all of us who loved my grandmother. At the age of ninety-six, she died peacefully after a long and wonderful life.

Grandma's friends and family gathered for a funeral Mass that was a real celebration of her life. My sister, four brothers, and I had all returned home to mourn the loss of a woman who had a remarkable influence on all of our lives. Although we had each journeyed down a different road in life, we were all united and connected by Grandma's love. Could Bobby understand that all of our tears came from the same place in each of our hearts? "I don't want you to be sad," was all he said.

I told Bobby that I was sad because we were saying good-bye to Grandma Kitty, and we would miss her. But I also told him that we should be happy because Grandma was going to heaven to be with Jesus. "Where is heaven?" Bobby asked. "I'm not really sure," I answered him. "It's a mystery. But Jesus made us a promise that we will be happy there and no one there will ever be sick or hurting again."

I heard Bobby tell his four-year-old friend Jilly that Grandma Kitty had died and gone to heaven. "I think heaven is like a sandy beach," Jilly said. "And it feels so good when you squish your toes in the sand in heaven."

In God's Words

Jesus said to her, "I am the resurrection and the life. Those who believe in me, even though they die, will live, and everyone who lives and believes in me will never die."

— John 11:25-26

"Very truly, I tell you, you will weep and mourn, but the world will rejoice; you will have pain, but your pain will turn into joy. . . . So you have pain now; but I will see you again, and your hearts will rejoice, and no one will take your joy from you."

— John 16:20, 22

Therefore we have been buried with him by baptism into death, so that, just as Christ was raised from the dead by the glory of the Father, so we too might walk in newness of life. For if we have been united with him in a death like his, we will certainly be united with him in a resurrection like his.

— Romans 6:4-5

What Can a Family Do?

1. Include special prayers for loved ones who have died.

2. Talk about the special memories you have of a family member who has died. Be open and honest with your children concerning questions of death, dying, and heaven.

3. Make a photo album with some of your family's favorite pictures of the deceased.

4. Plant a tree, donate money to a charity, or get involved in some living memorial that your loved one had a special interest in.

5. Remind your children that God shares our sorrow when someone we love dies, and God will help us through our sadness.

6. Let your children know it's okay to cry and to feel sad when a loved one has died. When Jesus learned that his friend Lazarus was dead, he was moved to tears even though he knew that death wasn't the end and that heaven awaited him.

How much do children understand about death, dying, and heaven? How much should parents tell them? Parents know their children's emotions and maturity better than anyone, and they should decide how to explain death and heaven to their children. But many times death catches us by surprise and we're not ready with the answers to the most difficult questions about life and death.

As parents, we have a responsibility to teach our children about death from a faith perspective, but it's a subject most of us aren't very comfortable with. Maybe it's because we don't have all the answers. Our own questions about heaven and eternal life are not all that different from our children's: Where is heaven? Is it up in the sky? Is there music there? Do we see things in color? How will we recognize each other without our earthly bodies? What will we do all day? It's great that everything will be so wonderful, but won't that ever get boring?

There are some outstanding books on death and dying for children that are available from most libraries. There are also books written to help children understand why God calls us home to heaven. But one of the most helpful explanations I heard came from a wonderful friend, Rev. Al Barrera, a Dominican priest who teaches theology and economics at Providence College in Rhode Island.

To be united with God and to share in the eternal happiness and love of God, that is heaven. But we don't have to wait to die to start enjoying heaven. Jesus gave us the first installment of heaven by teaching us how to love and to be loved.

The way Jesus preached, healed, and served—that was all giving us a taste of God's love for us. Now that He no longer walks the earth, it's up to us to continue building the Kingdom of God. When we reach out to help another person out of love and at the same time feel the love of God for us, that is already the beginning of heaven on earth. And it will come to its perfection when we meet God face to face.

We can teach our children that when we help someone in need, forgive a friend who has hurt us, or pray for peace in our world, the goodness we feel in our hearts is a glimpse of what we will all experience in heaven. As Father Al said, "It's heaven on earth."

A few nights after Grandma died, Bobby told me again that he didn't want to go to heaven. "I think you're going to have to talk to God about that," I told him. "Then I don't want you to listen," he said. He ducked under his covers and said, "God, I don't want to go to heaven, okay?" When he resurfaced I asked, "What did God say?" "He told me I didn't have to go." And thirty seconds later, having said his piece, he fell soundly asleep.

Books You Can Read with Your Children

Edna Eagle
by Gwen Costello

When Someone Dies: Children's Grief Workbook
edited by Joanne M. Pearring

What Happened When Grandma Died
by Peggy Barker

Badger's Parting Gifts
by Susan Varley

The Tenth Good Thing About Barney
by Judith Viorst

What On Earth Do You Do When Someone Dies?
by Trevor Romain

On the Wings of a Butterfly
by Marilyn Maple

My Grandpa Died Today
by Joan Fassler

The Fall of Freddie the Leaf
by Leo Buscaglia

When a Friend Dies: A Book for Teens About Grieving and Healing
by Marilyn E. Gootman

Bambi
by Walt Disney (Videotape from Disney)

Charlotte's Web
by E.B. White (Videotape from Paramount Home Video)

Wide Awake (Videotape)

Books and Resources for Parents

How to Go On Living When Someone You Love Dies
by Therese A. Rando, Ph.D.

A Grief Observed
by C.S. Lewis

Helping People Through Grief
by Delores Kuenning

What to Do When a Loved One Dies
by Eva Shaw

Mourning: The Journey From Grief to Healing
by Patrick DelZoppo

Answers to a Child's Questions About Death
(Guideline Publications)

The Gift of Peace
by Joseph Cardinal Bernardin

Welcoming Heaven: Prayers and Reflections for the Dying and Those Who Love Them
by Dr. J. Massyngbaerde Ford

Helping Children Cope with the Loss of a Loved One: A Guide for Grownups
by William C. Kroen, Ph.D.

Conversation Starters

1. What happens to nature during the fall? What do you notice happens in the spring?

2. It's important to me that in heaven I will find . . .

Prayer

Lord Jesus, you are the great giver of life and have triumphed over death. When we struggle over the difficult questions about life and death, help us to remember your promise of eternal life. When someone we love dies, remind us that you know the deep pain, sadness, and emptiness of losing a loved one and you will help us through our sorrow. Help us to comfort those who are grieving. And during our times of grief and loss, may the light of our risen Lord lead us out of the darkness, and fill us with hope and healing. Amen.

The Third Week of November

"Goodbye House"

The yellow "For Sale" sign hung on a white post in our front yard beckoning people to come inside our home. I looked at the sign many times during the time our house was on the market, and I knew that soon we would be leaving behind much more than a three bedroom brick Cape Cod house.

For thirteen years, Washington, D.C., had been my home. Soon after we were married, my husband, Joe, and I bought our house, a vessel holding the ordinary and extraordinary moments that have made up the life of our family. Joe and I were married in Washington, both of our children were born here, and we believed that our home would always be in the Washington area.

Then Joe was offered an exciting job opportunity in Princeton, New Jersey. The decision to leave behind a life we had known and loved was a difficult one. But as we talked about the possibilities of beginning a new chapter in our lives, we found that our fears of the unknown were gradually giving way to feelings of excitement and adventure.

We began getting our home ready to sell. "Get rid of all the clutter," we were advised. I was confused at this advice because the clutter was our lives. Everything that we packed or discarded was another reminder of the life we were leaving behind.

We were making great strides with our round-the-clock cleaning. We no longer needed a machete to get to our basement laundry room, and the roving pile of bills and mail was whittled down to a remarkable three pieces of paper. As we removed the dried Spaghettios from the kitchen baseboards, and the tire-sized dust balls from our closets, we hardly recognized our home.

One afternoon, there was a lunch for more than thirty real estate agents at our house. As I read their

In God's Words

By wisdom a house is built, and by understanding it is established; by knowledge the rooms are filled with all precious and pleasant riches.

— Proverbs 24:3-4

Your wife will be like a fruitful vine within your house; your children will be like olive shoots around your table.

— Psalm 128:3

O Lord, I love the house in which you dwell, and the place where your glory abides.

— Psalm 26:8

What Can a Family Do?

1. Talk with your children about your move openly and honestly. Express your sadness at leaving behind your home, special memories, and wonderful friends. Share your excitement about living in a new home, starting new memories and meeting new people.

2. Leave a special note in a secret hiding place in your home for the new owners to find. In the note describe a special memory you have of your home.

3. Put together a memory book of your favorite friends and places that you're leaving behind.

4. Say goodbye to your house—one room at a time.

Videotapes to Watch with Your Children

Far From Home—The Adventures of Yellow Dog from 20th Century Fox Family Features

Fly Away Home from the Columbia TriStar Family Collection

The Wizard of Oz from MGM Family Entertainment

Homeward Bound—The Incredible Journey from Walt Disney Productions

Homeward Bound II: Lost in San Francisco from Walt Disney Productions

Lassie Come Home from MGM Home Video

comments about our home, I became very defensive. I knew better than anyone that our house was small, that we lived on a busy street and that there were twenty-two steps from the street to our front door. But within our home's eight rooms, a family's life had been lived—memories had been made, arguments settled, children consoled, problems solved, and milestones celebrated.

One agent told me that our kitchen was cute, but very small. I didn't hear "cute" or "small" as she talked about my kitchen. Instead, I was taken back to an August evening three years earlier, when the electricity went out during a violent summer storm, and my children and I sat at the kitchen table and colored by candlelight. "The house is lovely," another remarked to me, "but that living room sure is tiny." I wanted to tell him about the night when twenty-seven neighbors filled that living room as we came together to help a friend who was diagnosed with cancer. My living room seemed enormous to me that evening. I wished I could have conducted my own house tour. Here is the family room where we celebrated my children's baptisms and birthdays. Here is the vegetable garden where my kids planted their first seeds. Here is the chair I cried in for two days after I miscarried, afraid that I might never have a child. And here are the steps I climbed the day I arrived home from the hospital with my children in my arms.

For many fall weekends, Joe and I frantically prepared for one open house after another. Those afternoons were especially unsettling to me because we were opening our house to complete strangers who saw our house the way it never looked—clean and empty! The real open houses had been held every day of the ten years we lived there, when our home was always open to friends, family, and neighborhood children. No contracts or warranties were ever needed to assure us of their love and support.

As we prepared to celebrate Thanksgiving that year, I felt especially blessed as I reflected on all God had given us during our years in Washington. This is the time of year when the weather turns cold, and we're reminded that there are far too many people in our city and country who will never have a home to call their own. Each morning in our country, more than one hundred thousand homeless children will wake up on shelter cots or city grates instead of in their own beds, in their own homes. Each night, more than seven hundred thirty-five thousand men, women, and children go to sleep without a hot meal or a warm bed. It's more than not having a roof over their heads. These forgotten families have no home in which to share their dreams, to build memories, and to create their own fabric of family life. This is perhaps the greatest injustice the homeless suffer.

One night, I read a book about moving to my children. It was the story of a little bear who tells his mama and papa that he has forgotten something inside his house after everything has been packed. His parents take him inside to say good-bye to each room of the house. "That's what I forgot," Little Bear says, "I forgot to say, 'Good-bye house.'"

On an unusually brisk November morning, we accepted an offer on our house. Our energies turned north. We knew that in a few weeks we would leave Washington full of heartache and hope as the memories, the experiences, and the people we love would remain forever in our hearts. And when we walked down our front steps for the last time, there was one thing I knew we would never forget to do. We turned around and said, "Good-bye house."

Books You Can Read with Your Children

Goodbye House
by Frank Asch

Alexander, Who's Not (Do You Hear Me? I Mean It!) Going to Move
by Judith Viorst

No Friends
by James Stevenson

The Berenstain Bears' New Neighbors
by Jan and Stan Berenstain

The Berenstain Bears' Moving Day
by Jan and Stan Berenstain

Cranberry Moving Day (Tales from Cranberryport)
by Wende and Harry Devlin

Oh, the Places You'll Go
by Dr. Seuss

A House Is a House for Me
by Mary Ann Hoberman

The Little House in the Big Woods (series) by Laura Ingalls Wilder

Books and Resources for Parents

Dave Barry's Homes and Other Black Holes
by Dave Barry

Sacred Dwelling
by Wendy Wright

Landscapes of the Soul
by Robert M. Hamma

Conversation Starters

1. What makes your home special?

2. Do you think we should help people who don't have a home? How?

Prayer

Blessing Before Moving From a Home

The leader may use these or similar words to introduce the blessing:

As we leave this home, we give thanks to God for all the blessings found here. We ask forgiveness for the wrong we have done one another. Let us pray that God will now guide us on our way.
God our refuge,
our home is ever with you.
May these rooms where we have lived
and found both joys and sorrows
be a place of blessing for those
who will live here after us.
Protect us on our way;
lead us to new friends;
help us to be a home to one another
and to all who need the love and shelter that is ours,
till at last we come to our eternal home with you.
Grant this through Christ our Lord.
Response: Amen.

(*Catholic Household Blessings & Prayers*, National Conference of Catholic Bishops, United States Catholic Conference)

The Fourth Week of November

National Family Caregiver's Week is observed during Thanksgiving Week.

"Grandma Kitty"

My then eighteen-month-old daughter, Teresa, strutted down the hall of the Lakeview Nursing and Rehabilitation Center as if she were the afternoon's entertainment rather than the youngest visitor to see her ninety-five-year-old Great-Grandma Kitty. Teresa poked her head in each patient's room, flashed a smile, wiggled her hips, and moved on.

As Teresa made her way down the hall, Grandma Kitty's eyes suddenly brightened, her smile returned, and she reached out playfully for her great-granddaughter. They laughed, they hugged, and Grandma Kitty even got a kiss. For a few minutes on a Saturday afternoon, it seemed that a child who was beginning to learn about her world and an elderly woman struggling to hold onto hers somehow realized they were connected. They knew they were family.

It had been four years since my grandmother, always the independent Irish woman, made the decision to leave her apartment in Florida where she had lived on her own since 1981. For the next three years, my parents cared lovingly and patiently for Grandma in their home. After two life-threatening falls and word from the doctor that she needed round-the-clock nursing care, my parents made the agonizing decision to place Grandma in a nursing home close to where they lived.

I saw firsthand how the family dynamics can change dramatically when an elderly parent moves in with a son or daughter. It is tough to see your own mother or father facing the physical, emotional, and financial demands of caring for an elderly parent in their home. My sister, my brothers, and I often felt frustrated because we all lived at least several hours away and couldn't provide the daily support that our parents deserved.

In God's Words

"I was sick and you took care of me. . . . Truly I tell you, just as you did it to one of the least of these who are members of my family, you did it to me."

— Matthew 25:36, 40

My child, help your father in his old age, and do not grieve him as long as he lives; even if his mind fails, be patient with him; because you have all your faculties do not despise him. For kindness to a father will not be forgotten.

— Sirach 3:12-14

What Can a Family Do?

The following is taken from *10 Tips for Family Caregivers* from the National Family Caregivers Association:

1. Choose to take charge of your life, and don't let your loved one's illness or disability take center stage.

2. Remember to be good to yourself. Love, honor, and value yourself. You're doing a very hard job and you deserve some quality time, just for you.

3. Watch for signs of depression and don't delay in getting professional help when you need it.

4. When people offer to help, accept the offer and suggest specific things they can do.

5. Educate yourself about your loved one's condition. Information is empowering.

6. There's a difference between caring and doing. Be open to technologies and ideas that promote your loved one's independence.

7. Trust your instincts. Most of the time they'll lead you in the right direction.

8. Grieve for your losses, and then allow yourself to dream new dreams.

9. Stand up for your rights as a caregiver and a citizen.

10. Seek support from other caregivers. There is great strength in knowing you are not alone.

When we were able to visit my parents, usually for holidays or family get-togethers, we realized that things had changed for all of us on these occasions. But for our parents, so had everyday life. I found myself wishing that Thanksgiving still meant that Grandma would be orchestrating the family dinner rather than asking to be served dinner alone in her room, unaware that a holiday was being celebrated. And I couldn't believe that it was just five years earlier that Grandma had kicked up her heels to "Hello Kitty" (sung to the tune of "Hello Dolly") on her ninetieth birthday in a restaurant filled with family and friends.

Illness, the loss of a spouse, and the loss of independence can all cause an elderly person to experience personality and behavioral changes, placing a great deal of stress and strain on caregivers as they struggle with their own feelings of anger, resentment, and guilt. This can be a painful and difficult time for the entire family, but it can also be a time of spiritual growth as our relationships with God and family are more closely examined. A caregiver understands that our faith calls on us to see that an elderly person at the end of her life should be treated with the same amount of dignity and respect as a child at the beginning of her life.

Still, meeting the daily needs of feeding, bathing, changing, and conversing with an elderly relative requires a great deal of patience and endurance. My mother has told me that caring for an elderly relative is a lot like caring for a child. She is quick to note this difference: when you devote your energies to a child, you look ahead and see a life full of hope and promise, but with an elderly person, you find yourself looking back. Although we believe that God will welcome our loved ones with open arms, the day-to-day existence for many elderly and their caregivers is often very painful.

As my father, my daughter, and I said our good-byes to Grandma that afternoon, I thought about how confused and sad her life had become. Still, she would surprise us at times. At times the memories of her family, her life, and especially her faith were powerful enough to triumph over her senility.

I walked back to Grandma, took hold of her freckled hand, and told her I loved her. "Did I ever tell you that you and Grandpa were the best grandparents anyone could ever have?" I asked her. She looked at me knowingly and said, "Well, we always tried our best." You did, Grandma, and your family will always love you for it.

What Can a Family Do?
(continued)

The National Family Caregivers Association (NFCA) is the only charitable organization dedicated to making life better for all of America's family caregivers. There are more than 25 million people who find themselves in a caregiving role. NFCA provides services in the areas of education, information, support, public awareness, and advocacy. NFCA is a membership organization and is open to anyone interested in supporting our nation's caregivers. Caregiver member services include "Take Care!" a quarterly newsletter for family caregivers, and many other special reports and educational materials. For more information, please call 1-800-896-3650. Internet: www.nfcacares.org

Books You Can Read with Your Children

The Wednesday Surprise
by Eve Bunting

Through Grandpa's Eyes
by Patricia MacLachlan

Saying Goodbye to Grandma
by Jane Resh Thomas

William and the Good Old Days
by Eloise Greenfield

My Grandmother's Stories: Collection of Jewish Folktales
by Adele Geras

Nana Upstairs & Nana Downstairs
by Tomie dePaola

Butterfly Boy
by Virginia L. Kroll

Grandmother and I
by Helen E. Buckley

Books and Resources for Parents

The Resourceful Caregiver: Helping Family Caregivers Help Themselves
by National Family Caregivers Association

Helping Someone with Mental Illness: A Compassionate Guide for Family, Friends, and Caregivers
by Rosalynn Carter

Laurel's Kitchen Caring: Recipes for Everyday Home Caregiving
by Laurel Robertson

A Loving Voice: A Caregiver's Book of Read-Aloud Stories for the Elderly
edited by Carolyn Banks and Janis Rizzo

Tuesdays With Morrie: An Old Man, A Young Man, and Life's Greatest Lesson
by Mitch Albom

The Educated Caregiver (Three-part video series) LifeView Resources, Inc. 1-800-395-LIFE (5433)

www.healthfinder.org (Healthfinder) Federal government's health web site

Conversation Starters

1. Can you remember a time when you were sick? Who were the people who helped you? What did they do to help you feel better?

2. How did Jesus care for those he met who were sick or dying? How does he tell us to care for the sick?

Prayer

O Lord, you are the great physician and healer. You have shown us the way to care for the sick in our families and communities. We pray for all families that are caring for a loved one who is ill. When these families feel it's almost impossible to go on, please give them your strength. It's not easy to care for a family member whose body, mind, and spirit are failing. They need patience, and they need time for themselves. May we reach out to these families and offer them a hot meal, help with errands, a few hours respite, or a shoulder to cry on. Help us to bring compassion to the sick and those who care for them. We ask this through Christ our Lord. Amen.

The First Week of December

The First Week of Advent

A Holy Night

On a Friday evening two weeks before Christmas, I stopped by to visit my friend Sister Josephine Murphy, the director of St. Ann's Infant and Maternity Home in Hyattsville, Maryland. Through its many programs, St. Ann's reaches out to homeless teenage mothers and provides a safe haven for abused and neglected children.

As we walked through the building's festively decorated halls, we heard the lively conversation of the young mothers as their babies ate next to them in a communal dining room. We listened to a loving volunteer soothing a crying newborn in a nursery filled with six babies in wooden cribs. We heard the protestations of three- and four-year-olds as clean-up time was underway. We listened to some of the devoted staff tell six toddlers parading around in Pampers that it was bath time. And as we passed one room, we heard the frightened cries of a young boy who had arrived a few days before. It was anything but a silent night, although in every way it was a holy night.

"You know, it does something to my whole insides when I think about what we're doing to our children today, " said Sister Josephine. "It seems that not enough people care about what's happening to kids. Somewhere along the line children have gotten in the way and we're paying a terrible price for how we've been treating our children. Believe me, children know when they're not wanted.

"We had one three-week-old boy who was brought to us after he was beaten up and thrown in a trash can. We took in a little girl who was in Children's Hospital for several months after being scalded by her mother and her mother's boyfriend. Two babies, six and eighteen months, were left

In God's Words

"Whoever becomes humble like this child is the greatest in the kingdom of heaven. Whoever welcomes one such child in my name welcomes me."

— Matthew 18:4-5

The spirit of the Lord God is upon me, because the Lord has anointed me; he has sent me to bring good news to the oppressed, to bind up the brokenhearted.

— Isaiah 61:1

"Do not be afraid; for see—I am bringing you good news of great joy for all the people: to you is born this day in the city of David a Savior, who is the Messiah, the Lord."

— Luke 2:10-11

What Can a Family Do?

1. Talk with your children about what it means to bring help to those in need. Discuss how you are already doing this as a family and what else you could do together.

2. As a family, organize or participate in a community drive to collect baby items for a home for unwed mothers and their babies. A collection for diapers and baby-wipes is especially helpful since these items are always needed.

3. As you light the candles on your Advent wreath, share one way that you will try to share the love and light of Jesus during the upcoming week, e.g., forgiving easily after an argument, making an effort to get along with a difficult person, showing patience with a brother or sister.

alone in an apartment for three days until a neighbor heard them crying. Both children came to us. Thank the Lord they are doing well now. We are destroying babies at six and seven months old through physical and sexual abuse and then we wonder why there are so many problems in our world today."

For the past five years, Sister Josephine has served at St. Ann's where she oversees a prenatal program for pregnant teenagers, a children's residential program for almost sixty children who have been abused, an adolescent mother-baby program, an accredited high school program, and a day care program.

As sister talked about the horror of child abuse, I couldn't help but wonder why such innocent children had to suffer so terribly and why so many teenage mothers were left abandoned with no place to go. It seemed a depressing and hopeless picture. Where was the message of Christmas to be found for children and young mothers like those at St. Ann's? How can we celebrate the joy of the birth of Jesus in the midst of such sorrow?

"The season of Christmas makes me ache even more for these children than I already do," said Sister Josephine. "It makes me talk to the Lord all the more and beg him to do something. I don't ever feel hopeless, but I do get angry and I try to channel that anger to talk to anyone who will listen to me about laws that need to be changed to protect our children. I will not hesitate to speak up on behalf of these children because it seems that no one else is doing it and these children have rights which must be protected. Besides, I still like a good fight!"

Sister Josephine explained that in many cases the girls who come to St. Ann's have been molested by their mothers' boyfriends and that's how they got pregnant. The mothers blame the daughters and tell them to get out of the house. "So we take them in," she said. "The mothers are on drugs and they're dragging down their teenage daughters with them. A lot of the children we see have been scarred by the effects of prenatal drug and alcohol abuse."

For almost all of their lives, many of these pregnant teenagers have been told they're good-for-nothings who will never amount to anything. But at St. Ann's, a group of committed sisters, staff, and volunteers work tirelessly to restore love, trust, and hope. St. Ann's also offers them a very good education. When these girls go to school they find out they have good minds. They also find that they can turn their lives around when they're given loving encouragement and warmth from someone who cares enough to listen. The high school at St. Ann's has a very high graduation rate among a group of girls who are mostly former dropouts. Some of the girls go on to college and many develop the necessary skills to get off of welfare and get into the job market.

"I often think of Adrianne," Sister Josephine said. "She was failing math and she needed to pass if she was going to receive her diploma. So Sister Joan got a volunteer tutor for Adrianne who worked with her round-the-clock it seemed. Well, the day she passed her math test and found out she was going to graduate, Adrianne ran into the office downstairs and got on the loudspeaker and announced to the entire building that she had passed the test. She had done it! We were all a part of that and everyone celebrated her victory."

As Sister and I continued our tour of St. Ann's, a teenager motioned to us as she picked up her four-day-old son dressed in pale blue terrycloth pajamas. "Come on over here, Sister Josephine. You have to see my little boy," beamed the proud young mother. She handed the infant to Sister Josephine who cuddled the crying baby and gently rocked him to sleep.

At Christmas, I think we are not only invited to come before the Child Jesus lying in a crib of hay but also to come before the cribs of the babies at places like St. Ann's and reach out to them. In the bruised and broken bodies of these children we are reminded that what lies at the heart of Christmas is a Child. We are also reminded that the Mother of this Child, like many of the mothers at St. Ann's, was a poor teenager without a home on the night her Son was born.

Books You Can Read with Your Children

December
by Eve Bunting

Young Claus: The Legend of the Boy Who Became Santa
by J. Michael Sims

The Christmas Miracle of Jonathan Toomey
by Susan Wojciechowski

Silver Packages: An Appalachian Christmas Story
by Cynthia Rylant

The Christmas Bird
by Bernadette Watts

The Best Christmas Pageant Ever
by Barbara Robinson

Papa's Angels
by Collin Wilcox Paxton and Gary Carden

The Christmas Tree
by Julie Salamon

The Christmas Story Book
collected by Ineke Verschuren

A Certain Small Shepherd
by Rebecca Caudill

Videotapes for the Christmas Season

A Charlie Brown Christmas
from Paramount Home Video

The Small One
from Walt Disney Mini Classics

Miracle on 34th Street
from Twentieth Century Fox

Rudolph the Red-Nosed Reindeer
from Family Home Entertainment

How the Grinch Stole Christmas
from MGM Home Video

The Little Drummer Boy
from Family Home Entertainment

Alvin and the Chipmunks: A Chipmunk Christmas
from Buena Vista Home Video

The Children's Circle (Christmas Stories)
from Early Advantage

The Nutcracker with Mikhail Baryshnikov (American Ballet Theater production)
from MGM Home Video

The Mouse in the Manger
(Book and Video) from Ave Maria Press

Conversation Starters

1. Do you think we should help people who are poor or homeless? Why or why not?

2. Why do some families suffer poverty, illness, or homelessness while others do not? Did God want it that way? Does he want us to notice, to help?

3. Were Mary and Joseph homeless on the night that Jesus was born? Why would God allow his Son to be born into poverty?

As we walk in the darkness of child abuse, violence, and homelessness today, we must have faith that the brilliant star that guided three kings to a baby in Bethlehem all those years ago can still lead us out of the darkness and into the light. And I can't help but think what a radiant angel the proud graduate Adrianne would be, heralding the news of the birth of Jesus to all those whose lives have been filled with the pain of child abuse, the anguish of abandonment, or the sorrow of substance abuse and poverty.

Prayer

Dear God, how we long to see your great light! Help us to remember that your Son was given to us to bring good news to all people. May we bring your light into the world as we reach out to the poor, the abused, and abandoned in our communities. During this Advent season open our hearts to the Christ Child and to all people in need, especially children. We ask this through Christ our Lord. Amen.

The Second Week of December

Hurry Up and Wait

My daughter, Teresa, was making up her own Christmas story when she was three years old. She had rearranged all the figures from the creche on top of our piano. Soon, three ceramic carolers, a wooden nutcracker, Frosty the Snowman, and Santa converged on her manger scene. Teresa then began an elaborate tale of a pretty angel, three kings on white horses, and a magic goose who tells the animals in the stable about the little baby Jesus. I knew my avid storyteller could appreciate the greatest story ever told so I sat down next to her and explained what really happened in a Bethlehem barn almost two thousand years ago. "Were there toys in the barn?" she asked me. "No, there were only animals," I answered. "Well, I would let Mary and Joseph and Jesus come into my house," she said. "And when Jesus got a little bigger, I would let him play with all my toys."

My son, Bobby, who was five at the time, overheard our conversation and gave Teresa a dose of reality. "Teresa, I'm sorry to tell you this but you can't let Mary and Joseph and Jesus in our house because they're all in heaven." Teresa forged on, "Then I will take a rocket ship to heaven." Bobby informed her that a rocket ship can only go as far as the moon. "Well then I'll fly on a plane to Bethlehem," she said.

As I listened to Bobby and Teresa, I couldn't help but think how open children are to bringing Jesus into their hearts at Christmas. Christmas is a season that children are comfortable with because Jesus comes to them on their level. Because children know what it's like to be little and sometimes misunderstood, they take the time to listen to the story of Jesus' birth, to ask questions about shepherds and stars, and to wonder why people would turn away a mommy, a daddy, and a baby boy.

In God's Words

Those who wait for the Lord shall renew their strength, they shall mount up with wings like eagles, they shall run and not be weary.

— Isaiah 40:31

Wait for the Lord; be strong, and let your heart take courage; wait for the Lord!

— Psalm 27:14

A voice cries out: "In the wilderness prepare the way of the Lord, make straight in the desert a highway for our God."

— Isaiah 40:3

What Can a Family Do?

1. Create family traditions during Advent that emphasize the Advent themes of waiting, preparing, and hoping.

2. As a family, light an Advent Wreath and talk about ways that you'll prepare for the coming of Jesus without getting swept up in the commercialism of Christmas.

3. Place an empty manger in a special place in your home. Fill a small basket with pieces of straw and put it next to the manger. Each time a family member does something good to prepare for Christ's coming, place a piece of straw in the manger. Try to have a full bed of straw by Christmas Eve.

4. Read Christmas stories that emphasize the importance of loving others and reaching out to people in need.

5. When you buy or make Christmas cookies, bring some to a lonely neighbor, a family in need, or a parishioner who is ill.

As often as we've heard the narrative of Christ's birth, the part of the story that seems to haunt adults and children through the ages is that no one could make room for a young mother-to-be and her husband. There was no room at the inn so our Messiah was born in a manger. How could anyone let this happen?

It's been almost two thousand years since the birth of our Lord and, like the shepherds and kings, we are searching for our Savior. But he is also seeking us. In our day, Mary and Joseph aren't knocking on the doors of high rise hotels, Jesus is knocking on the door of our hearts, wondering if we have room to bring him into our hurried and hectic lives. Jesus will not bang on our door or demand that we make room. He will wait for us patiently until we're ready to let him in.

It seems, at times, almost impossible to make room for Jesus in our busy lives. There are days when we're barely able to manage our own lives; how can we find the time for prayer, reflection, and work on the most important relationship in our lives? The Advent themes of patience, preparation, and longing seem out of step with our fast-paced world. Today's fascinating technologies—computers, laser printers, fax machines, cellular phones, etc.—provide us with up-to-the-minute communication and instant services. Today, we have more time-saving devices and less time than ever before.

We are a weary world that once again needs to become a waiting world. It's so important to be busy, productive, and to use the gifts and talents that God has given us. But we have become weary with the pressures, the demands, and the many stresses of life. During the season of Advent, Jesus asks us, "What are you so busy doing? Can you make room for me? I can bring you peace from your hectic life. I will give you the strength you need to get through the sorrows of your life."

When we follow the way of Jesus and fill our lives with love, forgiveness, and service to others, we become refreshed, restored, and renewed. No longer are we a people tired and discouraged. So long ago, there was no room for the Holy Family in the "place where travelers lodged." But today, whenever we serve a homeless family at a neighborhood shelter, spend a few minutes with a person who is lonely, forgive the seemingly unforgivable, or speak out against hatred and prejudice, we are saying that this year there is room at the inn.

At Christmas, my children help me to rediscover the wonder and joy of the birth of Jesus. The infant is a reminder that we can all begin again. It's never too late to start over. The real miracle of Christmas is that God sent us the gift of his Son to wash away our sins, to bring peace, to restore justice, to give everlasting love, and to offer the promise of eternal life to those who follow him. Christmas is a wonderful time to treasure this gift. We should let Jesus know that now, more than ever, we need him in our lives. We can let him know through prayer, through serving others, or by going to church more often. Or, like my daughter, Teresa, we can take the next plane to Bethlehem and let him know he's welcome in our homes this year. Merry Christmas!

Books You Can Read with Your Children

Advent Is for Children: Stories, Activities, Prayers
by Julie Kelemen

The Christmas Miracle of Jonathan Toomey
by Susan Wojciechowski

Silver Packages: An Appalachian Christmas Story
by Cynthia Rylant

Family Countdown to Christmas: A Day-by-Day Celebration
by Debbie Trafton O'Neal

Saint Francis Celebrates Christmas
Mary Caswell Walsh

The Real 12 Days of Christmas
by Helen Haidle

Books and Resources for Parents

A Way to the Heart of Christmas
edited by Brian Linard

The Gift of the Magi
by O. Henry

Too Much Holly, Not Enough Holy
by Patricia Wilson

Behold that Star: A Christmas Anthology
edited by Maria Arnold Maendel

Conversation Starters

1. In your life, what things do you have to wait for? Do you remember a time when you had to wait on line for a very long time? What was it like to wait that long?

2. If Jesus was born in Bethlehem two thousand years ago, why do we say we are still waiting for him during this season of Advent? What are we waiting for?

Prayer

Come, Lord Jesus, come into our hearts. Help us to receive the gift of patience. In our busy worlds, we don't like to wait. We have things to do, places to go, and people to see. In this season of Advent, may we slow down and remember that you are the one we are waiting for. May we prepare for your coming through prayer, loving service to those in need, and "turning to you with our whole heart." We ask this through Christ our Lord. Amen.

The Third Week of December

Blessed Bethlehem

One week before Christmas, Joe and I took our two children to a nearby church to visit a re-creation of the village of Bethlehem at the time of Christ's birth. More than eighty volunteers of a local drama ministry played the parts of the people of Bethlehem, complete with costumes, props, booths, and live animals. The Bethlehem village was true to the busy and bustling Bethlehem of two thousand years ago.

As we approached the village gate, three beggar children pleaded for food. A Roman soldier stood guard as each family was asked to register for the census. We wandered down the crooked streets of Bethlehem and were invited to play the part of visitors to this lively marketplace. We were tired and hungry from our long journey. An innkeeper informed us that there was no room at the inn, but we could purchase a tent for the night.

The people showed us their wares, their food, and their crafts. A carpenter worked on a wooden wheel. The proprietor of a fish and cheese shop showed us the catch of the day and gave the children a taste of goat cheese. We listened to the rabbi preach in the synagogue. A scribe gave my son, Bobby, a Hebrew letter on a stone. Two women at the well stopped gossiping long enough to offer my daughter, Teresa, a drink of water. As we strolled through the streets of Bethlehem, we were asked by all the people we met, "Did you see the bright star in the sky tonight? Have you heard that a king is to be born?"

As we were leaving the bustling village and beginning our journey home we thought we had been given a glimpse of what it might have been like on the night Jesus was born. Suddenly, we came across a simple stable where a woman, her husband, and a baby were kept warm by the breath of

In God's Words

Joseph also went from the town of Nazareth in Galilee to Judea, to the city of David called Bethlehem, because he was descended from the house and family of David. He went to be registered with Mary, to whom he was engaged and who was expecting a child. While they were there, the time came for her to deliver her child. And she gave birth to her firstborn son and wrapped him in bands of cloth, and laid him in a manger, because there was no place for them in the inn.

— Luke 2:4-7

They set out; and there, ahead of them, went the star that they had seen at its rising, until it stopped over the place where the child was.

— Matthew 2:9

What Can a Family Do?

1. Make a birthday card for Jesus or have a birthday cake as part of your Christmas celebration.

2. Participate in a "Giving Tree" through your parish or school as a reminder that Christmas is about giving to those in need.

3. Using the figures from your family's creche, ask your children to act out the Christmas story. Invite them to share their favorite part of the story.

4. Watch *A Charlie Brown Christmas* and talk about why Linus understood the real meaning of Christmas.

5. Visit a live nativity scene and ask your children to describe what they think the first Christmas was like.

Videotapes to Watch with Your Children

VeggieTales: The Toy That Saved Christmas
from Big Idea Productions

The Birth of Jesus (Visual Bible: Matthew)
from Monarch Home Video

A Charlie Brown Christmas
from Paramount Home Video

a donkey and a goat. Standing before this stark manger scene, I couldn't help but think that Jesus' life on earth, especially his birth, was a mystery.

As history hurries along, the story of Christ's birth becomes even more mysterious. We realize how far removed we are from the time and place of the birth of Jesus. Most of us have never met a shepherd. It's often difficult to spot a star—never mind a dazzling one—through the pollution of our city skies. We need to take a weekend ride to the country to see a stable, hay, and farm animals. We think of kings as antiquated figures from foreign lands and fairy tales.

Is it harder in our day to accept an immaculate conception, a virgin birth, a king born into poverty, or the union of the human and the divine? How do we make the mystery of Christ's birth come alive today?

The shelters and soup kitchens that offer a home and a hot meal to those who all others have turned away are our modern day stables. The inner city priest or sister who guides children and parishioners into the light of Christ are today's stars of wonder. All men, women, and children who trust in God and spread the good news with humility and simplicity are the shepherds of our time. A foster father who brings children into his home and loves them as his own is a present day Joseph. And a young woman who says yes to life, especially in a difficult pregnancy, follows in the footsteps of Mary at the manger. This is the real re-creation of the miracle of Bethlehem.

Perhaps the ultimate mystery is how God could love us so much that he would send his Son to a fallen world to be sacrificed for the forgiveness of our sins. As mysteries go, they don't get any bigger than this. How could anyone possibly love us this much? How can we possibly learn to love others this much?

Through faith, prayer, and loving service to others, we can get closer to uncovering the mystery of God's love and to understanding what a precious gift we were given on that first Christmas night. It is a gift of indescribable love, hope, and redemption.

As we set up the creches in our homes and churches may the stars, stables, and shepherds help us to stand in awe and wonder of the real mystery that began in the blessed village of Bethlehem: "When the angels had left them and gone into heaven, the shepherds said to one another: 'Let us go now to Bethlehem and see this thing that has taken place, which the Lord has made known to us.' So they went with haste and found Mary and Joseph, and the child lying in the manger. When they saw this, they made known what had been told them about this child" (Luke 2:15-17).

Books You Can Read with Your Children

The Christmas Angel
by Pirkko Vainio

Bright Christmas: An Angel Remembers
by Andrew Clements

This Is the Star
adapted by Joyce Dunbar

A Certain Small Shepherd
by Rebecca Caudill

The Christmas Story: According to the Gospels of Matthew and Luke
paintings by Gennady Spirin

The Very First Christmas
by Paul L. Maier

The Living Nativity
by David and Helen Haidle

Jacob's Gift
by Max Lucado

The Mouse in the Manger (Book and/or Video)
by Rev. Gennaro Gentile

The Christmas Story Book
collected by Ineke Verschuren

Books and Resources for Parents

The Promise
(Book and Compact disc)
by Michael Card

Conversation Starters

1. Where were you born? Ask your parents to tell you about the town where you were born.

2. Why do you think God chose Bethlehem as the birthplace for his Son?

Prayer

"O Little Town of Bethlehem"—the birth of your son in this bustling little village changed forever the course of human history. We ask that we will never lose our sense of wonder and awe of all that happened on that special night. Help us to re-create Bethlehem in our lives today by providing shelter to families in need, becoming stars of wonder to those without hope, serving as humble shepherds as we spread the good news. Help us to say yes to the miracle of life even in difficult circumstances. May the mystery and miracle of all that took place in the town of Bethlehem stay in our hearts throughout the year. We ask this through Christ our Lord. Amen.

The Fourth Week of December

The Season of Advent and Christmas

The Joy of Homecomings

One of my earliest childhood memories is of a certain Christmas Eve when Santa Claus came to our house. I was about four years old at the time and I remember telling my mother that Santa looked a lot like our next-door neighbor, Mr. Howland. But whatever doubts I had about Santa that night quickly disappeared as he said good-bye at our front door. "Where are your reindeer, Santa?" I asked. Without hesitation Santa replied, "Well, they're right there on your front lawn. It's hard to see them in the snow. But if you look over by that tree. . . ." As he opened the door and a gust of wind blew into our front hall, I stretched high on my tippy toes and for a fleeting moment, I spotted three reindeer standing near our birch tree.

If only we could hold on forever to the faith we had as children. It's a faith of openness, innocence, and awe that we wish we could recapture as adults. In the eyes of many children, the world is a place of wonder and marvel, where reindeer fly, where people are good, and where there is a God who watches over us all. Then one day we discover that Santa doesn't exist and Christmas is never quite the same. Children also learn—some much too early in life—that the world isn't always a safe place and there are more than a few people who do terrible things. So much of the goodness and mystery of life that we believe in as children has disappeared before we've reached adulthood.

I wonder if one of the reasons that so many people stop going to Church and believing in God is fear—fear that like so many other beliefs we've held over the years—this one too will be shattered. As one childhood belief after another is shot down, are we frightened that the belief we hold dearest—the one that sustains us when all others fail—will be

In God's Words

If a shepherd has a hundred sheep, and one of them has gone astray, does he not leave the ninety-nine on the mountains and go in search of the one that went astray? And if he finds it, truly I tell you, he rejoices over it more than over the ninety-nine that never went astray. So it is not the will of your Father in heaven that one of these little ones should be lost.

— Matthew 18:12-14

What Can a Family Do?

1. Talk with your children as they get older about the times you struggled with your faith. Let them know how important it is to be honest with God when they are praying. Sometimes it's okay to be angry with God.

2. If a friend or family member does not go to church, never make judgments about that person. Instead, invite them to church or a special event taking place at your church.

3. If you notice a new family or person coming to your church, introduce yourself and be welcoming.

4. Remember that many times a person has stayed away from the church because of past hurts. Listen to them and reassure them.

5. Many married couples who have recently become parents are interested in returning to church. Be open, welcoming, and supportive with them.

Videotapes for the Christmas Season

Miracle on 34th Street
(either version)
from Twentieth Century Fox

Rudolph the Red-Nosed Reindeer
from Family Home Entertainment

destroyed as well? We need to know that the birth, death, and resurrection of our Lord really did take place and that God's promise that he would send his Son to conquer sin and death is real.

I think many of us have had times in our lives when we've "fallen away" from our church and our faith. For a few years I didn't go to church, except at Christmas, Easter, and when I was home for the holidays visiting my parents. I don't think I ever stopped believing in God but my faith was slowly fading away. It was difficult to go to Christmas Mass at this time in my life. I felt awkward, sad, and disingenuous. It reminded me of the first Christmas I learned from a friend that there wasn't a Santa Claus. Still I pretended to believe so that the magic and miracle of this day wouldn't be lost forever.

After a time, I realized that God would use whatever faith I had and help me to understand that even though I had let go of God, he would never let go of me. And this is the message of Christmas: that God became human to save us all, no matter how low we've sunk or how far we've run away from him. God is a persistent and loving Father who wants us back. He knows the potential we have to touch the lives of others with his love and life and he won't give up on us that easily.

Christmas may be the only day of the year when a friend, neighbor, or family member goes to church. Those who have been away may feel uneasy stepping back into God's house. They may feel that it's been too long and they're simply going through the motions like many other holiday traditions. Let them know it's okay if they can't remember the words to all the prayers. God already knows what's in their hearts. It's important to remember that Jesus didn't come to those who had it all figured out. Jesus spent a lot of his ministry lifting up his friends and followers who often experienced doubt and denial. But these were the same people in whom Jesus entrusted the future of his church once they turned to him with their whole hearts.

In this Christmas season we celebrate the joy of homecomings. We celebrate the finding of the lost sheep—those lost to indifference, addiction, depression, and abuse but who were found by a steadfast and jubilant shepherd. Jesus' story of the Good Shepherd reminds us just how much God longs to have all his children back in his arms: "And when he comes home, he calls together his friends and neighbors, saying to them, 'Rejoice with me, for I have found my sheep that was lost.' Just so, I tell you, there will be more joy in heaven over one sinner who repents than over ninety-nine righteous persons who need no repentance" (Luke 15:6-7).

This Christmas Eve, if you've been away from the church, try to let your doubts disappear as you stand at your church's front door. "But where are you, Lord?" you may ask. Without hesitation he'll reply, "I'm here, right in front of you. Some days it's harder to see me. But if you look over here. . . ." Then open the door of your heart and let a gust of the Spirit's cool air blow into your life. Stretch high and look for the Infant Jesus. You'll find him whenever you reach out to the hungry, the thirsty, the sick, the poor, and powerless, the faithful, and the fallen away. And he will be real.

Books You Can Read with Your Children

The Polar Express
by Chris Van Allsburg

The Wild Christmas Reindeer
by Jan Brett

Red Ranger Came Calling: A Guaranteed True Christmas Story
by Berkeley Breathed

The Christmas Story Book
collected by Ineke Verschuren

The Life and Adventures of Santa Claus
by Julie Lane

Santa, Are You for Real?
by Harold Myra

Books and Resources for Parents

The Christmas Gift
by Emily Arnold McCully

The Christmas Box Collection
by Richard Paul Evans

The Return of the Prodigal Son
by Henri J. M. Nouwen

Conversation Starters

1. Why do some of our friends not go to church?

2. How should we talk about church to our friends who don't attend services?

Prayer

Faithful Shepherd, in your mercy and forgiveness you follow after all your lost sheep. You guide us on our journey and come after us when we've lost our way. Help us to share the mystery of our faith to those who have fallen away from you. Give us a child-like wonder so we may lead others back to you. May this Christmas season be a time of rejoicing and homecoming for all. We ask this through Christ our Lord. Amen.

Index

I

Illness	Third Week of February
Immigrants	Second Week of September
Independence	First Week of July
Injury	Fourth Week of January
Interfaith	Third Week of March

J

Journeys	Second Week of March, First Week of September
Joy	First Week of April
Justice	First Week of February

K

Kindergarten	First Week of August, First Week of September
Kindness	First Week of March, Third Week of April
Kingdom	Second Week of March

L

Laughter	First Week of April
Lent	First Week of March, Second Week of March
Letter Writing	Second Week of August
Listening	Third Week of August
Love	Second Week of February

M

Marriage	Second Week of February
Materialism	Fourth Week of August
Miracles	First Week of May
Miscarriage	Third Week of June
Mother	Second Week of January, Fourth Week of March, Second Week of May
Moving	First Week of January, Third Week of November
Mud Puddles	Third Week of May
Multi-culturalism	First Week of February, Second Week of September

N

Nature	Third Week of April, First Week of June
Needy	Fourth Week of June
Neighbors	First Week of January

O

Oklahoma City Bombing	Second Week of April

P

Parenting	Fourth Week of March
Patience	Second Week of December
Peace	Second Week of April, Second Week of July
Planet	Third Week of April
Playing	Third Week of May
Poor	Fourth Week of June
Prayer	Third Week of May, Fourth Week of September
Prejudice	First Week of February
Project Rachel	Third Week of January

Q

Quiet	Fourth Week of February

R

Racism	First Week of February
Religions	Third Week of March

S

Safety	Fourth Week of January
Saints	First Week of November
Santa Claus	Fourth Week of December
School	First Week of September, Fourth Week of October
Sea	Third Week of July
Security	Second Week of June
Sickness	Third Week of February, Fourth Week of November
Silence	Fourth Week of February
Simpler Life	Fourth Week of August